MOTHER TELLS YOU HOW

This is a Prion Book

First published in the UK in 2007 by Prion
An imprint of the Carlton Publishing Group
20 Mortimer Street
London W1T 3JW

ISBN: 978-1-85375-617-7

The publishers would like to thank David Abbott at IPC for all his help in compiling this book.

Edited and compiled by Lorna Russell

Art director: Lucy Coley
Design: design@timpattinson.com
Production: Janette Burgin

CONTENTS

INTRODUCTION

Launched in 1951 under the banner 'the New Super Colour Weekly for Every Girl', *Girl*, with its combination of adventure tales, advice, competitions, fashion ideas and pin-ups, provided inspiration and guidance for half a million teenage girls in Britain throughout the fifties.

Very much of its time, 'Mother Tells You How' was one of the paper's most popular and longest-running strips. Each week Mother would teach her exemplary-in-every-way daughter, Judy, one of life's essential skills, such as how to decorate biscuits, how to use old cheese or how to make an umbrella cover.

Where *Girl*'s more famous companion paper for boys, *Eagle*, featured new inventions and clever conjuring tricks, *Girl* had Mother telling Judy how to make a shelf-tidy. *Eagle* subscribers read about shark fishing off the coast of Australia, while their sisters would turn to 'Mother Tells You How' for wise words on how to care for goldfish.

   Girl readers weren't to have their little heads filled with science they didn't understand,

conjuring tricks for show-offs and tales of danger on the high seas. They were kept busy

sorting out their small odds and ends into a homemade shelf-tidy, and experimenting

with unusual sandwiches.

   'Mother Tells You How' appears to be an over-the-top '50s spoof,

but is in fact a wholly genuine period piece. There is no irony here,

and it's the well-intended, earnest instruction that provides such

high comedy in our very different times.

1

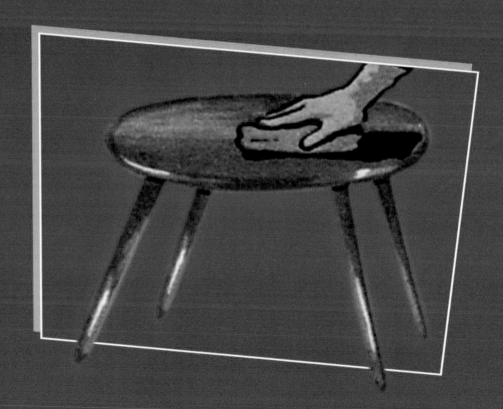

MOTHER TELLS YOU HOW

TO MAKE A LAUNDRY BAG

10

MOTHER TELLS YOU HOW

TO WASH LACE

THE LACE COLLAR DADDY BROUGHT ME FROM BRUSSELS IS RATHER DIRTY, MOTHER. HOW DO I WASH IT?

REAL LACE NEEDS CAREFUL HANDLING, JUDY. I'LL SHOW YOU WHAT TO DO.

NEVER LET LACE GET REALLY DIRTY

FIRST OF ALL, GIVE THE COLLAR A GOOD SHAKE. THEN MAKE A SOAPY LATHER WITH LUKEWARM WATER.

SOAP FLAKES

HALF FILL A SCREW-TOP JAR WITH THIS SOAPY WATER. THEN PUT IN THE COLLAR AND SCREW THE LID ON THE JAR.

SHAKE THE JAR VIGOROUSLY, THEN LEAVE IT FOR A SHORT TIME.

NOW RINSE THE COLLAR IN THREE LOTS OF WARM WATER. FINALLY, DIP IT INTO A BOWL OF THIN STARCH.

STARCH

SPREAD THE COLLAR OUT ON A THICK TOWEL PINNING IT INTO SHAPE. COVER IT UP AND LEAVE IT TO DRY. IRONING IS QUITE UNNECESSARY.

THERE, MOTHER — MY COLLAR LOOKS LIKE NEW!

MOTHER TELLS YOU HOW

TO DO THE
WASHING UP

> SCRAPE OFF ALL BITS OF FOOD, JUDY, THEN STACK THE DISHES NEATLY.

KNIFE HANDLES MUST BE KEPT OUT OF WATER OR THEY WILL SOON BECOME DISCOLOURED. ALWAYS WASH THE CLEANEST THINGS FIRST—FOR INSTANCE: GLASSES, THEN CUTLERY, THEN CUPS AND SAUCERS. PLATES AND DISHES LAST.

> STAND THE CUTLERY IN A JUG OF HOT SOAPY WATER.

> PUT THE 'DIRTIES' ON THE LEFT OF THE SINK, JUDY, AND A BOWL OF CLEAN HOT WATER ON THE RIGHT FOR RINSING.

KEEPING TIDY AND CLEARING UP AS YOU GO ALONG MAKES THE TASK SO MUCH EASIER. RINSE EVERYTHING BEFORE DRYING AND KEEP A CLOTH HANDY FOR SAUCEPANS SO THAT YOU DON'T HAVE TO WIPE THEM ON THE TEA TOWEL.

> USE PLENTY OF HOT WATER AND A SMALL AMOUNT OF DETERGENT. A LONG-HANDLED MOP IS ALWAYS USEFUL AND WILL PREVENT YOUR HANDS FROM GETTING RED AND SORE.

> THAT'S RIGHT, JUDY—PUT EVERYTHING AWAY AS YOU WIPE.

SOME PEOPLE PREFER NOT TO WIPE CROCKERY BUT JUST TO RINSE IT IN HOT WATER AND THEN LEAVE IT TO DRY IN RACKS. IT'S A GOOD IDEA BUT NOT A VERY TIDY ONE IF THE KITCHEN IS SMALL.

> I POLISHED THE SILVER WITH A DRY CLOTH BEFORE PUTTING IT AWAY.

GIVING THE SILVER A DAILY RUB OVER SAVES A LOT OF *REAL* CLEANING AND, IF IT IS PUT AWAY IN STRICT ORDER, YOU CAN KEEP A CHECK ON IT AND SEE THAT NO ODD PIECES GET LOST.

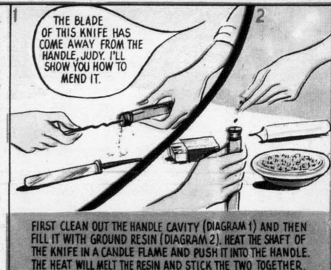

MOTHER TELLS YOU HOW

TO MAKE A

Matching Table Set

MOTHER, CAN'T WE HAVE A REALLY MODERN TABLE SET?

YES, JUDY, WE'LL MAKE ONE FROM THE VERY LATEST MATERIALS.

RYDURA IS A SOFT MATERIAL AND RYMALITE IS A PATTERNED HARDBOARD. BOTH ARE MADE IN THE SAME PATTERNS AND ARE WASHABLE AND HEATPROOF.

FOR 4 PLACE MATS AND 6 HEAT-PROOF MATS YOU WILL NEED:— 7/8 YARD OF RYDURA (FOR THE PLACE MATS), A PIECE OF RYMALITE MEASURING 3FT BY 8INS, FELT FOR BACKING, WHITE ADHESIVE, LACQUER FOR EDGES.

FELT

ADHESIVE

CUT THE RYDURA AND FELT INTO MATS, 15 INCHES BY 10 INCHES, THEN STICK THEM TOGETHER.

PINKING SHEARS.

PINK ALL ROUND THE EDGE. IF YOU LIKE, YOU CAN QUILT THE MATS BY STITCHING THEM IN SQUARES.

FELT.

WHITE ADHESIVE.

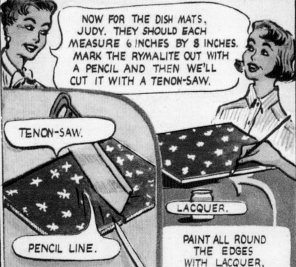

NOW FOR THE DISH MATS, JUDY. THEY SHOULD EACH MEASURE 6 INCHES BY 8 INCHES. MARK THE RYMALITE OUT WITH A PENCIL AND THEN WE'LL CUT IT WITH A TENON-SAW.

TENON-SAW.

PENCIL LINE.

LACQUER.

PAINT ALL ROUND THE EDGES WITH LACQUER.

OH, JUDY, WHAT A LOVELY COLOUR SCHEME!

ISN'T IT NICE? AND ALL THE MATS CAN BE SPONGED CLEAN, TOO.

MOTHER TELLS YOU HOW

TO LAY A TABLE

FOR BREAKFAST, JUDY, USE GAY CHINA ON A COLOURED CLOTH. IT'S BEST TO LAY THE TEA OR COFFEE THINGS ON A TRAY TO THE RIGHT OF THE POURER.

BREAKFAST IN BED IS A LUXURY. JUDY'S MOTHER TOLD HER TO MAKE THE TRAY LOOK AS ATTRACTIVE AS POSSIBLE AND BE QUITE CERTAIN SHE HADN'T FORGOTTEN ANYTHING. THE FINISHING TOUCH—A SINGLE FLOWER IN A TINY VASE.

THERE'S COTTAGE PIE FOR LUNCH TODAY, JUDY, AND WE'LL HAVE FRUIT AFTERWARDS.

FOR A SIMPLE MEAL LIKE THIS USE LINEN PLACE MATS WITH MATCHING NAPKINS. THESE ARE EASY TO WASH, NEED LITTLE IRONING.

WHICH WOULD YOU LIKE, MOTHER—CAKE OR BISCUITS?

AFTERNOON TEA, LAID ON A TRAY CLOTH, SERVED FROM A TROLLEY, SAVES A LOT OF WORK AND THE TROLLEY CAN BE WHEELED WHEREVER YOU PLEASE.

THE TABLE DOES LOOK NICE, JUDY!

WHEN GUESTS ARE COMING TO DINNER, BRING OUT ALL THE BEST CHINA AND GLASS AND USE THE PRETTIEST PLACE MATS. A SHALLOW BOWL OF FLOWERS MAKES AN ATTRACTIVE CENTRE-PIECE.

MOTHER TELLS YOU HOW

TO MAKE A REMINDER BOARD

OH, MOTHER, I CAN'T FIND MY TICKET FOR THE CLUB CONCERT ANYWHERE.

WE NEED A REMINDER BOARD! LET'S MAKE ONE TOGETHER.

CHOOSE A 12 INCH SQUARE OF FAIRLY STOUT CARD-BOARD TO MATCH YOUR HALL OR KITCHEN.

THIS BRIGHT-COLOURED BOARD WILL DO.

NOW WE'LL CUT V SHAPES ON IT, LIKE THIS, JUDY.

USE A RAZOR BLADE IN A HOLDER OR A VERY SHARP PENKNIFE. BEND THE V s FORWARD SLIGHTLY.

THERE, IT'S FINISHED. NOW WE CAN FIX IT UP.

TO FIX THE BOARD TO THE WALL, YOU CAN EITHER HANG IT ON A CORD, OR, IF THE SURFACE IS TILED, STICK IT IN POSITION WITH ADHESIVE TAPE AT THE CORNERS.

NO MORE LOST SHOE-REPAIR TICKETS, OR CLEANING VOUCHERS, JUDY! WE'LL KEEP ALL THAT SORT OF THING HANDY ON OUR REMINDER BOARD.

16

MOTHER TELLS YOU HOW

TO IRON A BLOUSE

I WISH I COULD IRON MY BLOUSES SO THAT THEY LOOKED LIKE NEW, MOTHER.

I'LL SHOW YOU THE RIGHT WAY, JUDY, AND THEN THEY WILL!

FIRST, SPRINKLE WATER ALL OVER THE BLOUSE TO BE IRONED.

IT'S NO USE TRYING TO IRON A GARMENT UNLESS IT HAS BEEN THOROUGHLY DAMPENED.

NOW FOLD THE GARMENT, PULLING COLLARS AND CUFFS INTO SHAPE, THEN ROLL IT UP TIGHTLY IN A CLEAN TOWEL SO THAT IT BECOMES EVENLY DAMP ALL OVER.

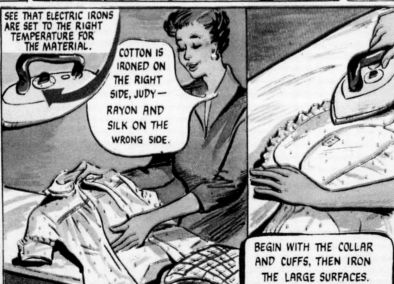

SEE THAT ELECTRIC IRONS ARE SET TO THE RIGHT TEMPERATURE FOR THE MATERIAL.

COTTON IS IRONED ON THE RIGHT SIDE, JUDY — RAYON AND SILK ON THE WRONG SIDE.

BEGIN WITH THE COLLAR AND CUFFS, THEN IRON THE LARGE SURFACES.

THIS BLOUSE LOOKS AS CRISP AND NEAT AS A NEW ONE NOW, MOTHER!

MOTHER TELLS YOU HOW

TO STORE WINTER CLOTHES

MOTHER, I WON'T NEED THESE THICK THINGS ANY MORE THIS YEAR.

NO, JUDY. WE'LL STORE THEM RIGHT AWAY AND SAVE SPACE IN YOUR WARDROBE AND CHEST.

FIRST MAKE CERTAIN THAT EVERYTHING IS QUITE CLEAN. WASH WOOLLENS AND HAVE SUITS AND COATS CLEANED BEFORE STORING.

WASHING

DRY CLEANING

NOW WE'LL FOLD THE WOOLLENS NEATLY AND PACK THEM IN POLYTHENE BAGS.

POLYTHENE BAGS.

RUBBER BAND

USE GOOD SIZED BAGS, SO THAT THE ENDS CAN BE CLOSED TIGHTLY BY TWISTING RUBBER BANDS ROUND THEM.

COATS AND SUITS ARE BEST HUNG UP IN POLYTHENE WARDROBES OR LARGE BAGS.

THAT'S RIGHT, JUDY. LET US HOPE YOU HAVEN'T GROWN OUT OF EVERYTHING BY THE AUTUMN!

MOTHER TELLS YOU HOW

TO DEAL WITH DRAUGHTS

MOTHER — THERE'S AN AWFUL DRAUGHT FROM MY WINDOW.

WE'LL SOON STOP THAT, JUDY.

A ROLL OF PLASTIC FOAM DRAUGHT-STOPPING, PLEASE.

THIS IS SOLD IN 20 FT. ROLLS AND IS SELF-STICKING.

NOW, JUDY, YOU HOLD THE ROLL WHILE I STICK IT IN POSITION.

PRESS THE ADHESIVE EDGE FIRMLY ALL ROUND THE WINDOW FRAME.

CUT

THAT'S RIGHT. NOW CUT OFF THE END — WE'LL USE THE REST TO GO ROUND THE DOOR FRAME.

PUT THE STOPPING ON THE DOOR FRAME, NOT THE DOOR.

OH, MOTHER, WHAT A DIFFERENCE THERE IS, NOW THAT DRAUGHT HAS GONE.

MOTHER TELLS YOU HOW

TO DEAL WITH MOTHS

THERE'S MOTH IN THIS CORNER OF THE SPARE ROOM CARPET, JUDY. I'LL SHOW YOU HOW TO DEAL WITH IT.

LAY A DAMP TOWEL OVER THE INFECTED PART AND THEN IRON IT DRY WITH A HOT IRON. THIS KILLS EGGS AND GRUBS.

TO MAKE QUITE SURE WE'LL SPRINKLE SOME PARADICHLORBENZENE CRYSTALS BETWEEN SHEETS OF NEWSPAPER AND PUT THEM UNDER THE WHOLE CARPET.

PARADICHLORBENZENE DISCOURAGES MOTH IN ALL STAGES. SPRINKLE IT IN GAPS BETWEEN THE SKIRTING AND THE FLOORBOARDS, AND ANY PLACES WHERE FLUFF IS LIKELY TO COLLECT.

BEFORE WE PUT OUR WINTER CLOTHES AWAY WE'LL SEE THAT THEY ARE WELL BRUSHED AND HAVE NO GREASY SPOTS.

MOTHS LOVE GREASY SPOTS — SO SEE THAT ALL STORED CLOTHES ARE QUITE CLEAN.

PUT ENVELOPES CONTAINING CRYSTALS IN OUR WINTER BOOTS, JUDY. DON'T FORGET TO PUNCH HOLES IN THE PAPER.

ALSO HANG PERFORATED PAPER BAGS OF PARADICHLORBENZENE CRYSTALS AMONG THE CLOTHES IN STORAGE CUPBOARDS AND WARDROBES.

SPREAD NEWSPAPER, WITH THE CRYSTALS BETWEEN, ON THE TOPS OF TRUNKS AND BLANKET CHESTS.

THAT'S A GOOD JOB DONE! NOTHING TO WORRY ABOUT NOW.

MOTHER TELLS YOU HOW

TO PREPARE A ROOM FOR A GUEST

AUNT MARY WANTS TO SPEND THE NIGHT WITH US, JUDY. WE MUST GET THE SPARE ROOM READY!

GUESTS ARE USUALLY TIRED IF THEY HAVE COME ON A LONG JOURNEY, SO TRY TO PREPARE EVERYTHING BEFOREHAND SO THAT THERE IS NO 'FUSS AND BOTHER' WHEN THEY ARRIVE.

GOODNESS, WHAT A MESS!

YES—AND I'M ALWAYS *BEGGING* EVERYONE NOT TO STORE THINGS THEY DON'T WANT IN THIS ROOM.

A ROOM THAT ISN'T OFTEN USED IS FREQUENTLY UNTIDY, SO FIRST CLEAR IT OUT AND THEN GIVE IT A THOROUGH CLEANING. YOU'LL NEED BED-CLOTHES FOR THE BED—AND DON'T FORGET AN EXTRA BLANKET IN CASE YOUR GUEST IS COLD.

WE'LL OPEN THE WINDOWS WIDE, JUDY, SO THAT THE ROOM IS WELL AIRED.

JUDY'S MOTHER HAS PUT UP SOME FRILLY CURTAINS TO GIVE THE ROOM A FRESH, WELCOMING LOOK—

—AND JUDY HAS ADDED A FRESH BEDCOVER, AN EIDER-DOWN AND THE BEDSIDE RUG FROM HER OWN ROOM.

HERE'S A HOT-WATER BOTTLE IN CASE AUNT MARY HAS FORGOTTEN HERS.

THE BEDSIDE TABLE ON ONE SIDE SHOULD HOLD FLOWERS, A CARAFE OF WATER, BOOKS AND MAGAZINES; ON THE OTHER, A LAMP.

THE ROOM LOOKS MUCH MORE COMFORTABLE NOW AND I DON'T THINK WE'VE FORGOTTEN ANYTHING.

A List of 'Musts'

TIDY ROOM.

WELL AIRED BED.

EXTRA BLANKET.

HOT-WATER BOTTLE.

BEDSIDE LAMP.

WATER AND GLASS.

FLOWERS.

BOOKS.

MAGAZINES.

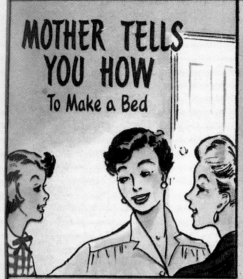

MOTHER TELLS YOU HOW
To Make a Bed

COME AND WATCH WHILE AUNTIE KITTY AND I MAKE THIS BED THE CORRECT WAY, JUDY.

WHEN YOU FIRST GET OUT OF BED, ALWAYS REMEMBER TO TURN BACK THE BED-CLOTHES NEATLY AND OPEN THE WINDOW WIDE SO THAT THE ROOM IS WELL AIRED.

NOW YOU'VE TAKEN OFF THE UNDER SHEET AND BLANKET, JUDY, WE CAN TURN THE MATTRESS.

TURN THE MATTRESS OVER TOP TO TAIL. DOING THIS ONCE A WEEK EVENS OUT THE WEAR AS WELL AS ADDING TO YOUR COMFORT. WHEN THIS IS DONE, PUT BACK THE BLANKET AND UNDER SHEET.

THE PILLOW MUST BE SHAKEN AND THE SHEET TUCKED ROUND THE BOLSTER.

THE SHEET SHOULD BE PERFECTLY SMOOTH AND REALLY TIGHT OR THERE'LL BE UNCOMFORTABLE CREASES TO LIE ON.

NOW FOR THE TOP SHEET. WATCH CAREFULLY— THIS IS AN ENVELOPE CORNER.

THERE ARE THREE MOVES. (1) TUCK SHEET ROUND END OF MATTRESS IN THE ORDINARY WAY. (2) FOLD THE CORNER OF SHEET UNDER SEPARATELY. (3) TUCK IN OVERLAPPING FLAP AS SHOWN ABOVE IN THE ILLUSTRATIONS. FOLD BLANKETS IN THE SAME WAY.

WHEN YOU HAVE TUCKED IN THE BED-CLOTHES ALL ROUND, TURN THE SHEET NEATLY OVER THE TOP OF THE BLANKETS TO STOP THEM FROM TICKLING YOUR FACE.

THERE YOU ARE, JUDY, YOU CAN DO IT BY YOURSELF NEXT TIME.

NEATNESS AND COMFORT GO HAND IN HAND WHERE BED-MAKING IS CONCERNED. IF YOU CAN GET SOMEONE TO SHARE THE JOB WITH YOU, IT WILL SAVE A LOT OF TIME AND ENERGY.

MOTHER TELLS YOU HOW

To Keep Your Room Clean

OH, MOTHER, I DO HOPE MY NEW RUG WON'T GET DIRTY TOO QUICKLY.

I'LL SHOW YOU HOW TO SPRAY IT SO THAT IT WON'T.

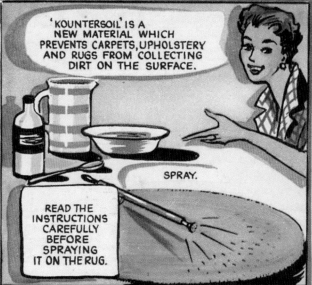

'KOUNTERSOIL' IS A NEW MATERIAL WHICH PREVENTS CARPETS, UPHOLSTERY AND RUGS FROM COLLECTING DIRT ON THE SURFACE.

SPRAY.

READ THE INSTRUCTIONS CAREFULLY BEFORE SPRAYING IT ON THE RUG.

YOU CAN SPRAY NEW CHAIR-COVERS IN THE SAME WAY.

SPRAY

LINO AND TILES WILL KEEP CLEAN AND SHINING FOR A LONG TIME IF TREATED WITH SILICONE WAXES.

THESE NEW WAXES NEED VERY LITTLE RUBBING.

YOUR ROOM ALWAYS LOOKS SO CLEAN, JUDY.

MOTHER TELLS YOU HOW

TO KEEP COOL

YOU'LL BE MUCH COOLER, JUDY, IF YOU TAKE OFF THAT TIGHT BELT.

CELLULAR WEAVE IN COTTON, WOOL OR REAL SILK IS THE COOLEST MATERIAL TO WEAR AS IT IS POROUS AND ABSORBENT. CHOOSE LOOSE-FITTING SHAPES AND AVOID TIGHT BELTS, NECK-BANDS OR CUFFS.

FOOD IS VERY IMPORTANT IN HOT WEATHER. GREEN SALADS, FRUIT, ICES AND COLD DRINKS *LOOK* COOLER AND THEREFORE MAKE ONE *FEEL* COOLER. BUT EAT PLENTY—ESPECIALLY MEAT, EGGS AND CHEESE—AS HOT DAYS CAN BE VERY EXHAUSTING.

DON'T OVERDO THE SUNBATHING, JUDY. YOU'LL ONLY PEEL AND LOOK HORRID.

SUNBATHE A LITTLE AT A TIME UNTIL YOU ARE QUITE BROWN. REMEMBER THAT HEATSTROKE, NOT SUNSTROKE, IS THE DANGER. AVOID GETTING VERY HOT, THEN VERY COLD—AND DON'T USE UP LOTS OF ENERGY CYCLING OR PLAYING TENNIS IN THE HEAT OF THE DAY.

CLOSE ALL WINDOWS AND DRAW THE CURTAINS BEFORE THE SUN STARTS BEATING DOWN ON THE HOUSE. OPEN THEM WHEN THE SUN GOES OFF IT AGAIN.

WE'VE ONLY JUST OPENED UP.

THAT MUST BE WHY IT'S SO BEAUTIFULLY COOL IN HERE!

MOTHER TELLS YOU HOW

TO DO THE FLOWERS

THE FIRST RULE IS TO CHOOSE FLOWERS WHICH ARE NOT IN FULL BLOOM, JUDY.

THIS IS IMPORTANT WHETHER YOU BUY FLOWERS IN THE SHOPS OR PICK THEM IN YOUR OWN GARDEN. QUITE TIGHT BUDS WILL COME OUT IN WATER AND LAST MUCH LONGER.

TO ARRANGE FLOWERS PROPERLY YOU'LL NEED A FIRM FOUNDATION OF SOME KIND. CRUMPLED-UP WIRE-NETTING IS IDEAL FOR WIDE BOWLS OR TALL VASES. USE SAND OR MOSS FOR SMALL BOWLS. ALWAYS STRIP THE LEAVES FROM THE STALKS WHICH WILL BE UNDER WATER.

OH DEAR, THESE FLOWERS HAVE DROOPED TERRIBLY, MOTHER. WHAT CAN I DO WITH THEM?

TO REVIVE FLOWERS WITH SAPPY STEMS, SUCH AS TULIPS AND ANEMONES, CUT THE STEMS UNDER WATER WITH A SHARP KNIFE OR SCISSORS (DIAGRAM 1). WOODY STEMMED FLOWERS LIKE ROSES AND LILAC SHOULD BE HAMMERED (DIAGRAM 2) OR HAVE THE OUTER COVERING SCRAPED OFF FOR AN INCH OR TWO (DIAGRAM 3). TULIPS SHOULD BE WRAPPED IN PAPER AND STOOD IN A TALL GLASS OF WATER — AN ASPIRIN WILL OFTEN HELP (DIAGRAM 4).

FILL UP THE BOWLS WITH WATER EVERY DAY. IF THERE'S A FIRE IN THE ROOM, TAKE THE FLOWERS OUT AT NIGHT — BUT REMEMBER TO KEEP THEM AWAY FROM DRAUGHTS.

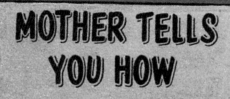

MOTHER TELLS YOU HOW

TO MAKE POMANDERS

MOTHER, WHAT IS A POMANDER? THIS STORY TALKS ABOUT THEM.

IT'S AN ORANGE OR LEMON STUCK WITH CLOVES. I'LL SHOW YOU HOW TO MAKE SOME, JUDY.

CHOOSE SMALL THIN SKINNED FRUIT AND GOOD CLOVES WITH LONG STALKS.

CLOVES

WE'LL DO THE ORANGES FIRST. STICK THE CLOVES ALL OVER, BUT LEAVE BANDS ROUND THE MIDDLE FOR A HANGING RIBBON.

THIS IS FUN! I'M MAKING A PATTERN ON MINE.

NOW DO THE LEMONS IN THE SAME WAY. KEEP THE CLOVES QUITE CLOSE TOGETHER.

WHEN YOU HAVE FINISHED, PUT ALL THE FRUIT TO DRY IN A COOL PLACE.

2 MONTHS LATER

WE CAN TRIM OUR POMANDERS NOW, JUDY. THEY ARE ALL QUITE DRY.

OOH, WHAT A NICE SMELL, JUDY!

TIE RIBBON ROUND THE 'UNSTUCK' BANDS AND MAKE LOOPS FOR HANGING, AS IN THE PICTURES. POMANDERS GIVE A DELIGHTFUL SCENT TO CLOTHES AND LINEN AND ARE LOVELY JUST TO SMELL.

MOTHER TELLS YOU HOW

TO DEAL WITH FOUR PROBLEMS

WE MUST GET RID OF THE FAT IN THIS SOUP STOCK, JUDY. WE HAVEN'T TIME TO WAIT FOR IT TO COOL.

WRING OUT A CLEAN CLOTH IN COLD WATER AND FOLD IT TO MAKE SEVERAL THICKNESSES. LINE A CULLENDER WITH THIS AND POUR THE STOCK THROUGH IT. THE FAT WILL CONGEAL ON THE WET CLOTH.

MOTHER, THIS LOAF IS MUCH TOO STALE TO EAT FOR TEA.

DON'T WORRY, WE'LL SOON PUT THAT RIGHT.

BREAD

HOLD THE LOAF UNDER THE TAP SO THAT IT IS WET ALL OVER. THEN POP IT INTO A HOT OVEN AND BAKE FOR TEN MINUTES.

ROBIN IS MAKING A FUSS ABOUT TAKING HIS COD LIVER OIL, MOTHER.

HERE, ROBIN, OPEN YOUR MOUTH FOR THIS LOVELY BULL'S-EYE.

GIVE YOUNGSTERS A STRONG PEPPERMINT SWEET *BEFORE* THE MEDICINE, THEN THEY WON'T NOTICE.

OH, JUST LOOK AT MY BLOUSE! I'VE SCORCHED IT DOWN THE FRONT.

GRANNIE'S SCORCH MIXTURE WILL SOON DEAL WITH THAT.

SCORCH MIXTURE

PEEL, SLICE AND POUND UP AN ONION, THEN MIX IT WITH HALF A PINT OF VINEGAR, 2 OZS. OF WASHING SODA AND 2 OZS. OF FULLER'S EARTH. BOIL ALTOGETHER FOR ABOUT TEN MINUTES. STRAIN AND, WHEN COOL, BOTTLE THE MIXTURE. SPREAD THIS OVER THE SCORCH MARK AND LEAVE TO DRY. REPEAT UNTIL THE MARK DISAPPEARS, THEN REWASH.

LOOK, MOTHER. YOU WOULD NEVER KNOW IT HAD BEEN SCORCHED!

NO, DEAR—BUT NEXT TIME DON'T FORGET TO TEST THE IRON FIRST.

MOTHER TELLS YOU HOW

TO TREAT CUTS AND BURNS

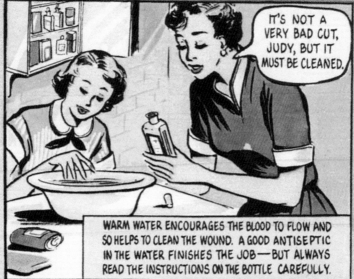

IT'S NOT A VERY BAD CUT, JUDY, BUT IT MUST BE CLEANED.

WARM WATER ENCOURAGES THE BLOOD TO FLOW AND SO HELPS TO CLEAN THE WOUND. A GOOD ANTISEPTIC IN THE WATER FINISHES THE JOB—BUT ALWAYS READ THE INSTRUCTIONS ON THE BOTTLE CAREFULLY.

KEEP IT COVERED UP, JUDY, AND IT WILL HEAL IN NO TIME!

TO COVER THE CUT USE A STRIP OF BORACIC LINT, THE SMOOTH SIDE NEXT TO THE CUT, THEN A PIECE OF BANDAGE TO KEEP IT IN PLACE.

OW!—THAT HANDLE AGAIN! I HAVE BURNT MY FINGERS BADLY THIS TIME.

BAKING POWDER

BAKING POWDER MADE INTO PASTE WITH WATER AND PUT ON BURNS *AT ONCE* NOT ONLY SOOTHES BUT MAKES A GOOD FIRST AID DRESSING. NEVER BREAK BLISTERS.

NO MORE BURNS FOR ME! I'VE COVERED THE HANDLE WITH THIN PLASTIC-COVERED WIRE.

SAUCEPAN OR KETTLE HANDLES OFTEN GET TOO HOT IF THE GAS IS LEFT ON HIGH. STRING BOUND ROUND THEM CAN BE USED INSTEAD OF THE PLASTIC.

First Aid List

Thermometer
Gauze bandages in several widths
Adhesive bandages
Packet of lint
Packet of cotton-wool
Lotion for sunburn
Iodine
Sal volatile
Disinfectant
Aspirin
Cough linctus
Inhalant

AREN'T WE A COUPLE OF CRIPPLES? BUT PROMPT TREATMENT MEANS A QUICK CURE!

THE MOST IMPORTANT THING ABOUT MINOR ACCIDENTS IS TO DEAL WITH THEM AT ONCE. IF THERE IS ANY DOUBT AT ALL, CALL IN YOUR DOCTOR.

MOTHER TELLS YOU HOW

TO BATH THE BABY

IS EVERYTHING READY FOR BABY'S BATH, JUDY? AND HAVE YOU TESTED THE HEAT OF THE WATER?

BE SURE THAT EVERYTHING YOU NEED IS READY FOR THE BATH BEFORE YOU PICK BABY UP. WATER MUST BE 'ELBOW' TEMPERATURE AND NO MORE. CLEAN EYES, NOSE AND FACE WITH SEPARATE PIECES OF COTTON-WOOL.

HOLD BABY FIRMLY, JUDY, LIKE THIS AND LOWER HIM INTO THE WATER. IT'S IMPORTANT THAT HE FEELS QUITE SECURE ALL THE TIME.

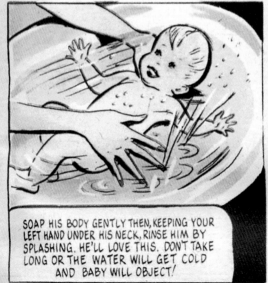

SOAP HIS BODY GENTLY THEN, KEEPING YOUR LEFT HAND UNDER HIS NECK, RINSE HIM BY SPLASHING. HE'LL LOVE THIS. DON'T TAKE LONG OR THE WATER WILL GET COLD AND BABY WILL OBJECT!

THERE WE ARE! NOW LIFT HIM ON TO YOUR LAP WHICH HAS A TOWEL ALL READY FOR PATTING HIM DRY.

HE LIKES YOU TO TALK TO HIM ALL DURING THE BATH, JUDY, EVEN THOUGH HE'S VERY YOUNG.

BATH-TIME ROUTINE SHOULD BE SMOOTH AND REASSURING FOR BABY. THAT'S WHY EVERY-THING SHOULD BE READY TO HAND FIRST. THINGS YOU'LL NEED ARE TOWELS, CHAFING CREAM, CLOTHES, NAPPIES, COTTON-WOOL, SOAP, SAFETY PINS, HAIR-BRUSH, POTTY, AND TALCUM POWDER TO DRY HIM THOROUGHLY BEFORE DRESSING.

MOTHER TELLS YOU HOW

TO BABY-SIT

LOTS OF MY FRIENDS BABY-SIT, MOTHER, AND JILL'S AUNT HAS ASKED ME TO DO IT FOR HER NEXT WEEK, BUT I'VE NEVER DONE IT BEFORE.

IT'S REALLY QUITE EASY, JUDY, BUT THERE ARE ONE OR TWO USEFUL TIPS TO REMEMBER.

IT IS VERY IMPORTANT TO MAKE FRIENDS WITH THE BABY SOME TIME BEFORE YOU TAKE CHARGE.

THEN, BEFORE THE PARENTS LEAVE, MAKE SURE YOU KNOW:
1—EXACTLY WHERE THEY ARE GOING AND THE TELEPHONE NUMBER, IF POSSIBLE.
2—THE TIME THEY WILL BE BACK.
3—THE TELEPHONE NUMBER OF A NEIGHBOUR OR RELATION TO CALL IN AN EMERGENCY.

BABIES AND YOUNG CHILDREN SELDOM WAKE UP IN THE NIGHT, JUDY. BUT IF THEY DO, A QUIET WORD OF REASSURANCE WILL GENERALLY SEND THEM TO SLEEP AGAIN.

GOOD NIGHT, JIMMY — SLEEP WELL!

YOU NEEDN'T WORRY ABOUT GETTING HOME NOW, JUDY. MY HUSBAND WILL GO WITH YOU. WE'VE HAD A WONDERFUL TIME, THANKS TO YOU!

MOTHER TELLS YOU HOW

TO WASH BABY'S CLOTHES

EVERY DAY IS BABY'S WASHING DAY, JUDY, FOR YOU MUST NEVER LET DIRTY CLOTHES PILE UP.

HAVE TWO 'NAPPY' PAILS HALF FILLED WITH WATER—ONE FOR THE DIRTY ONES AND ONE FOR THE WET ONES. PUT THE NAPPIES IN AS SOON AS THEY'RE TAKEN OFF AND LEAVE TO SOAK. WASH THEM WITH PURE SOAP FLAKES AND RINSE WELL UNDER RUNNING WATER.

DRYING OUT-OF-DOORS KEEPS WHITE THINGS A GOOD COLOUR AND MAKES THEM SMELL SWEET, JUDY.

BOIL NAPPIES AND COTTON GARMENTS EVERY FOUR OR FIVE WASHES. TAKE CARE IN THE RINSING AND ALWAYS USE AT LEAST TWO FRESH LOTS OF WATER—ONE HOT, ONE COLD.

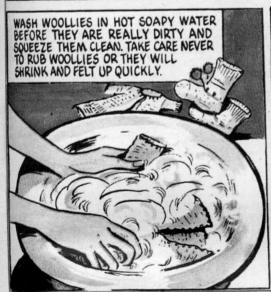

WASH WOOLLIES IN HOT SOAPY WATER BEFORE THEY ARE REALLY DIRTY AND SQUEEZE THEM CLEAN. TAKE CARE NEVER TO RUB WOOLLIES OR THEY WILL SHRINK AND FELT UP QUICKLY.

DON'T LEAVE WOOLLIES TO SOAK. WASH THEM, RINSE THEM AND DRY THEM AS QUICKLY AS POSSIBLE. HANG OUT IN THE OPEN WHENEVER YOU CAN. LITTLE HANGERS HOOKED INTO THE PEGS WILL DRY THE WOOLLIES QUICKLY AND IN GOOD SHAPE.

PRESS WOOLLIES LIGHTLY WITH A WARM IRON. TOWELLING NAPPIES SHOULD BE IRONED OR MANGLED SO THAT THEY ARE SOFT AND SMOOTH.

WE MUST MAKE QUITE SURE EVERYTHING IS WELL AIRED BEFORE WE PUT IT AWAY, JUDY.

MOTHER TELLS YOU HOW

TO FEED A TODDLER

"WILL YOU GIVE ROBIN HIS LUNCH TOMORROW, JUDY? I'LL SHOW YOU HOW TO DO IT TODAY."

"LOVELY, MUMMY! I'LL TAKE HIM AWAY TO WASH HIS HANDS BEFORE SITTING HIM DOWN."

"HERE'S HIS FEEDER. HE WILL HAVE THE SAME FOOD AS WE DO, BUT IT MUST BE MASHED UP SMALL."

GOOD HABITS ARE FORMED AT THE TODDLER STAGE, SO IT IS IMPORTANT TO MAKE BABY'S MEALS ORDERLY AND REGULAR.

"MASH UP THIS BAKED HADDOCK WITH SOME POTATOES AND CAULIFLOWER, JUDY, AND ADD A GOOD DAB OF BUTTER. LET HIM FEED HIMSELF, BUT TIDY UP THE PLATE FOR HIM SO THAT HE EATS IT ALL UP."

WHENEVER POSSIBLE IT IS BETTER FOR THE TODDLER TO EAT THE SAME FOOD AS THE FAMILY, THEN HE DOESN'T FEEL RESENTFUL AND MAKE A NUISANCE OF HIMSELF.

"IF HE PLAYS WITH HIS MILK PUDDING BEFORE FINISHING IT UP, JUDY, JUST TAKE IT AWAY FROM HIM GENTLY."

EACH CHILD KNOWS HIS OWN CAPACITY AND IT IS WRONG TO FORCE FOOD ON HIM. THERE IS NO NEED TO WORRY THAT A HEALTHY CHILD WILL EVER STARVE HIMSELF.

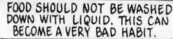

"NOW FOR HIS DRINK OF MILK — KEEP IT UNTIL LAST."

FOOD SHOULD NOT BE WASHED DOWN WITH LIQUID. THIS CAN BECOME A VERY BAD HABIT.

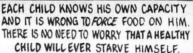

LITTLE CHILDREN NEED A GREAT DEAL OF ENCOURAGEMENT AND ASSURANCE, SO ALWAYS TELL THEM WHEN THEY DO WELL.

"COME AND BE WASHED, ROBIN — YOU *DID* EAT UP NICELY!"

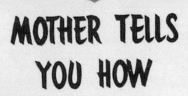

MOTHER TELLS YOU HOW

TO LOOK AFTER YOUR BUDGERIGAR

WHAT A LOVELY PRESENT, JUDY. YOU MUST LEARN HOW TO LOOK AFTER HIM PROPERLY.

BUDGERIGARS ARE QUITE EASY TO KEEP HEALTHY AND HAPPY, BUT THEY DO NEED REGULAR AND INTELLIGENT ATTENTION.

FOOD
MIX YOUR OWN
1 part of small canary seed.
½ part of yellow millet.
½ part of white millet.
A few whole clipped oats.

IN ADDITION
Grit and cuttle-fish bone. In summer give small quantities of chickweed, groundsel and seeding grasses. In winter give small pieces of lettuce, spinach, carrot or apple.

BE CAREFUL TO SEE THAT GREEN-STUFF IS QUITE FRESH AND WELL WASHED.

NO CAKES SUGAR or BISCUITS

HIS TRAY MUST BE CLEANED AND SANDED EVERY OTHER DAY.

GIVE HIM FRESH WATER EVERY DAY, JUDY. ONCE A WEEK ADD A FEW DROPS OF TINCTURE OF IODINE TO KEEP HIM FIT.

ALLOW THREE DROPS TO A WINEGLASS OF WATER.

BUDGERIGARS LIKE TO SPLASH ABOUT IN A WATER TROUGH, SO GIVE THEM A SHALLOW, WIDE ONE.

TOYS

A MIRROR AND A BELL ARE THE TOYS FOR YOUR BUDGERIGAR. HE WILL ALSO LIKE A LITTLE LADDER TO RUN UP AND DOWN.

JUDY, JUDY, PRETTY JUDY!

COCK BIRDS SOON LEARN TO TALK — HEN BIRDS TAKE LONGER. ONE PERSON ONLY SHOULD ATTEMPT TO TRAIN THEM, SPEAKING TO THEM SOFTLY AND CLEARLY.

MOTHER TELLS YOU HOW

TO CARE FOR GOLDFISH

LOOK WHAT I WON AT THE FETE, MOTHER.

IMPORTANT FISH SHOULD NEVER BE KEPT IN BOWLS. THE SURFACE AREA IS TOO SMALL TO ALLOW ENOUGH OXYGEN TO BE TAKEN IN.

GOLDFISH! WE MUST GET THE PROPER AQUARIUM EQUIPMENT FOR THEM AT ONCE.

WE SHALL NEED A TANK, SAND (OR GRAVEL), AND WEEDS, JUDY — AND A BOOK ON HOW TO FEED THE FISH.

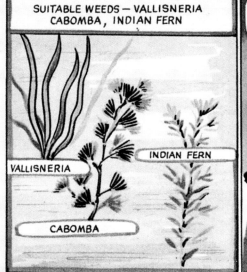

SUITABLE WEEDS — VALLISNERIA CABOMBA, INDIAN FERN

VALLISNERIA

INDIAN FERN

CABOMBA

WASH THE SAND OR GRAVEL, AND LAY IT ON THE BOTTOM OF THE TANK.

PLANT THE WEEDS IN GROUPS, AND PUT IN A FEW BIG SHELLS.

FILL UP THE TANK VERY GENTLY. MAKE SURE THAT THE WATER IS CLEAR AGAIN BEFORE PUTTING IN THE FISH.

WHEN FEEDING YOUR FISH, FOLLOW THE BOOK'S INSTRUCTIONS *EXACTLY*.

WE'LL PAINT ONE SIDE GREEN, AND THEN WE CAN HAVE THE TANK ON THE WINDOW-SILL.

MOTHER TELLS YOU HOW

TO FEED BIRDS IN WINTER

DON'T THE BIRDS LOOK MISERABLE IN THIS COLD WEATHER, MOTHER?

YES, JUDY. HARD FROST ALWAYS MEANS A SHORTAGE OF FOOD AND WATER FOR THEM, BUT WE CAN DO SOMETHING TO HELP.

PUT A SHALLOW BASIN OF WATER WELL OUT OF THE WAY OF CATS AND DOGS AND REMEMBER TO REPLACE THE WATER IF IT FREEZES.

THIS WILL DO FOR THE WATER. I'VE PUT A FEW STONES IN THE BOTTOM FOR THE BIRDS TO PERCH ON.

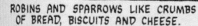

ROBINS AND SPARROWS LIKE CRUMBS OF BREAD, BISCUITS AND CHEESE.

MAKE A WIRE COIL, FILL IT WITH MONKEY NUTS, AND HANG FROM A BRANCH. WHENEVER POSSIBLE, KEEP THE BIRDS' FOOD OFF THE GROUND.

HALF A COCONUT WILL BE POPULAR WITH THE BLUE TITS.

HANG BACON RINDS AND BONES WITH BITS OF GRISTLE ON THEM FROM THE BOUGHS OF TREES.

LOOK AT THE BIRDS NOW, MOTHER! THEY'RE HAVING A WONDERFUL TIME!

2

MOTHER ON
ARTS AND CRAFTS

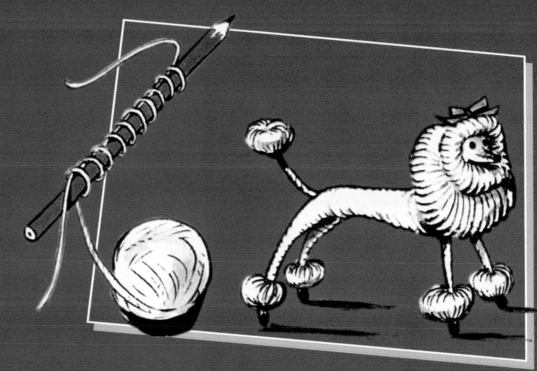

MOTHER TELLS YOU HOW

TO MAKE "SPATTER PATTERN" BOOK-PLATES

WHAT CAN I DO, MOTHER? I HAVE LOST TWO MORE OF MY BOOKS THROUGH LENDING THEM TO PEOPLE.

WHY NOT STICK IN BOOK-PLATES, JUDY, SO THAT THE BORROWER KNOWS THE BOOK BELONGS TO YOU? YOU CAN MAKE THE PLATES YOURSELF.

CUT OUT A SIMPLE SHAPE IN CARDBOARD—SUCH AS A LEAF, A FISH OR A FLOWER. LAY THIS ON TO A SHEET OF PAPER, WHICH CAN BE WHITE OR COLOURED, AND THEN "SPATTER" THE PATTERN.

TO DO THIS, DIP A TOOTH-BRUSH IN POSTER PAINT, OR COLOURED INK, AND THEN DRAW A KNIFE OVER THE TOOTH-BRUSH TO MAKE IT "SPATTER" ALL ROUND THE PATTERN. DO THIS SEVERAL TIMES, SO THAT THE SHAPE IS OUTLINED THICKLY WITH SPOTS. LEAVE UNTIL DRY.

THIS BOOK BELONGS TO *JUDY BLAKE*

NOW TAKE OFF YOUR PATTERN AND WRITE IN THE UNSPATTERED PART "THIS BOOK BELONGS TO..." (ADD YOUR NAME).

NOW STICK THE BOOK-PLATE ON THE FRONT PAGE OF EACH OF YOUR BOOKS AS A REMINDER THAT YOU ARE THE OWNER.

GREETINGS

A.E
R.T
FROM ME

Best Wishes

"SPATTER PATTERNS" CAN BE USED TO MAKE GREETING CARDS OF ALL KINDS, AND LOOK VERY EFFECTIVE IF YOU CHOOSE CONTRASTING PAPER AND PAINT.

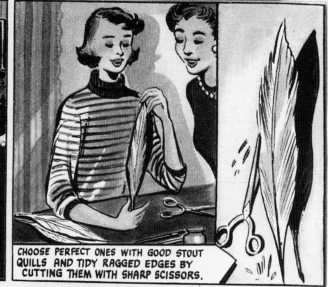

MOTHER TELLS YOU HOW

TO MAKE PIPE CLEANER POODLES

MOTHER, WHAT CAN I MAKE QUICKLY FOR THE CLUB BAZAAR?

PIPE CLEANER POODLES ARE ALWAYS POPULAR. I'LL SHOW YOU HOW TO DO THEM.

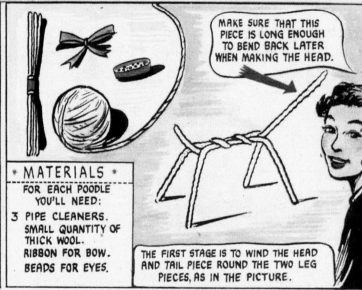

MAKE SURE THAT THIS PIECE IS LONG ENOUGH TO BEND BACK LATER WHEN MAKING THE HEAD.

* MATERIALS *

FOR EACH POODLE YOU'LL NEED:

3 PIPE CLEANERS. SMALL QUANTITY OF THICK WOOL. RIBBON FOR BOW. BEADS FOR EYES.

THE FIRST STAGE IS TO WIND THE HEAD AND TAIL PIECE ROUND THE TWO LEG PIECES, AS IN THE PICTURE.

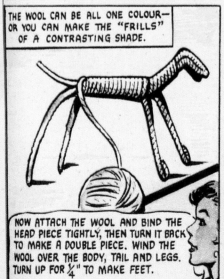

THE WOOL CAN BE ALL ONE COLOUR—OR YOU CAN MAKE THE "FRILLS" OF A CONTRASTING SHADE.

NOW ATTACH THE WOOL AND BIND THE HEAD PIECE TIGHTLY, THEN TURN IT BACK TO MAKE A DOUBLE PIECE. WIND THE WOOL OVER THE BODY, TAIL AND LEGS. TURN UP FOR ¼" TO MAKE FEET.

MAKE "FRILLS" FOR THE LEGS, FACE AND TAIL BY WINDING THE WOOL ROUND A PENCIL OVER A THREAD, THEN SLIPPING OFF THE LOOPS AND TYING THEM IN PLACE. PAINT THE NOSE BLACK AND SEW ON THE BEADS FOR EYES.

THOSE POODLES DO LOOK PRETTY, JUDY! CAN I HAVE THREE, PLEASE?

BAZAAR

MOTHER TELLS YOU HOW

TO MAKE AN UMBRELLA COVER

DOESN'T THAT UMBRELLA LOOK PRETTY, MOTHER? I *WOULD* LIKE A COVER FOR MINE.

Mannequin PARADE

HERE'S YOUR "COVER," JUDY! DAD NEVER WEARS IT AND IT'S REAL SILK.

ANY GOOD TIE WILL MAKE AN UMBRELLA COVER. UNPICK THE LABEL AND, IF NECESSARY, WASH THE TIE CAREFULLY AND PRESS IT LIGHTLY.

NOW WE'LL TAKE OUT THE INNER LINING. IT'S GENERALLY ONLY TACKED IN.

LEAVE IN THE PLAIN, ALL-OVER LINING WHICH IS OFTEN FOUND IN GOOD SILK TIES.

CUT THE TIE TO FIT THE LENGTH OF YOUR UMBRELLA, ALLOWING FOR THE WIDE END TO COVER THE TOP OF THE SPOKES. MAKE A TINY HEM ALL ROUND THE BOTTOM. CUT A STRIP FROM THE NARROW, LEFT-OVER PART OF THE TIE, NEATEN THE EDGES AND SEW A BUTTON ON ONE END AND A LOOP ON THE OTHER. THIS SHOULD FIT TIGHTLY ROUND THE NECK OF THE COVER TO KEEP IT IN PLACE ON THE UMBRELLA.

WHAT A LOVELY UMBRELLA COVER, JUDY!

MOTHER TELLS YOU HOW

To Make PLANT POT COVERS

OH THANK YOU, JUDY—WHAT A LOVELY PRIMULA! I MUST MAKE A PRETTY COVER FOR THE POT. WILL YOU BRING ME THE RAFFIA FROM THE TOOL SHED?

CHOOSE SIX STRANDS OF EVEN THICKNESS AND TIE THEM TOGETHER. NOW PLAIT THEM TIGHTLY, JOINING IN NEW STRANDS AS YOU NEED THEM.

IT IS BEST TO USE A LENGTH OF PREPARED RAFFIA FOR THE SEWING UP.

FOR THE SIDES OF THE COVER, MAKE A PLAIT ABOUT SIX YARDS LONG AND SEW IT IN THE SAME WAY, BUT WORKING ROUND AND ROUND TO FIT THE POT.

SEW THE BASE TO THE SIDES AND FINISH OFF THE POT RIM WITH A THICK PLAIT MADE OF 9 OR 12 STRANDS OF RAFFIA.

ANY SIZE COVER CAN BE MADE IN THE SAME WAY. TO PREVENT DAMP COMING THROUGH ON TO THE SILL, PUT A TIN LID INSIDE THE COVER FOR THE POT TO STAND IN.

WHEN YOUR PLAIT IS ABOUT ONE AND A HALF YARDS LONG, MAKE THE BASE OF THE POT BY COILING IT ROUND AND ROUND AND SEWING THE PLAIT TOGETHER AT THE EDGES.

BASE

42

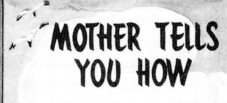

MOTHER TELLS YOU HOW

TO MAKE A RAFFIA HAT

JUDY, WHAT ABOUT MAKING A BRIM-HAT FOR THE HOLIDAYS? WE'LL USE NATURAL-COLOURED RAFFIA.

BRIM-HATS ARE VERY FASHIONABLE AND GREAT FUN TO WEAR ON THE BEACH.

BEGIN BY MAKING A PLAIT, USING NINE STRANDS OF RAFFIA. YOU WILL NEED SEVERAL YARDS, SO ROLL THE PLAIT INTO A BALL AS YOU GO ALONG.

RAFFIA PLAIT

NOW SEW IT ROUND AND ROUND LIKE THIS.

BEGIN THE BRIM BY MAKING A CIRCLE TO FIT YOUR HEAD. NOW, USING NARROW RAFFIA AND A PACKING NEEDLE, SEW THE STRIP ROUND AND ROUND (WORKING INTO THE HOLES, NOT THROUGH THE RAFFIA).

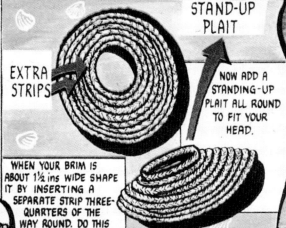

EXTRA STRIPS

STAND-UP PLAIT

NOW ADD A STANDING-UP PLAIT ALL ROUND TO FIT YOUR HEAD.

WHEN YOUR BRIM IS ABOUT 1½ ins WIDE SHAPE IT BY INSERTING A SEPARATE STRIP THREE-QUARTERS OF THE WAY ROUND. DO THIS TWICE, THEN THE BACK WILL BE ABOUT 1½ ins NARROWER THAN THE FRONT AND SIDES.

FOR FUN, TIE A SCARF OVER YOUR HEAD BEFORE PUTTING ON YOUR BRIM-HAT.

MOTHER TELLS YOU HOW

TO MAKE A JEWEL BOX

YOUR FATHER HAS JUST SMOKED THE LAST OF HIS CHRISTMAS CIGARS, JUDY, SO YOU CAN HAVE THE BOX TO MAKE A JEWEL CASE.

OH THANKS, MOTHER! MY THINGS GET INTO AN AWFUL TANGLE IN MY DRAWER.

FIRST OF ALL RUB THE BOX SMOOTH WITH FINE SANDPAPER, THEN GIVE IT TWO COATS OF LACQUER PAINT, LEAVING THE INSIDE OF THE LID AND THE BOTTOM UNPAINTED.

SCARLET VELVET WILL LOOK VERY RICH WITH THE ROYAL BLUE PAINT.

CUT VELVET AND LINING TO FIT THE LID AND BOTTOM, ALLOWING AN EXTRA ¾" ALL ROUND.

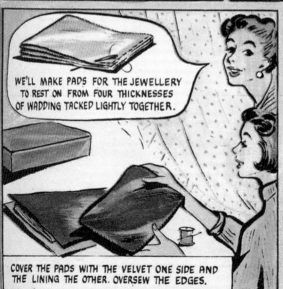

WE'LL MAKE PADS FOR THE JEWELLERY TO REST ON FROM FOUR THICKNESSES OF WADDING TACKED LIGHTLY TOGETHER.

COVER THE PADS WITH THE VELVET ONE SIDE AND THE LINING THE OTHER. OVERSEW THE EDGES.

STICK THE PADS INTO POSITION, LINING DOWNWARDS, ON THE BOTTOM OF THE BOX AND ON THE LID.

THIS GOLD BRAID WILL GIVE THE PERFECT FINISHING TOUCH. STICK IT NEATLY ALL ROUND THE EDGES OF THE LID SO THAT IT FITS INTO THE BOX.

OH, JUDY, WHAT A LOVELY JEWEL BOX YOU'VE MADE!

MOTHER TELLS YOU HOW

To Make a Matchbox Jig saw Puzzle

MOTHER, WHAT CAN I DO WITH THESE MATCHBOXES I'VE COLLECTED?

YOU CAN USE SOME FOR CHRISTMAS PRESENTS.

LITTLE CHILDREN LOVE PUZZLES. YOU CAN MAKE A LOVELY PRESENT FOR 3 TO 6 YEAR OLDS WITH MATCHBOXES.

THESE CALENDAR PICTURES WILL BE EXCELLENT.

MARK OUT ON THE BACKS OF THE PICTURES LIKE THIS. THEN CUT OUT THE PIECES AND STICK THEM FIRMLY ON BOTH SIDES OF THE BOXES.

FINALLY, ADD A COAT OF CLEAR VARNISH.

FOR A SUPER PRESENT, PUT A TINY GIFT IN EACH BOX.

JILL, DO YOU THINK YOUR LITTLE SISTER WILL LIKE ONE OF THESE?

MOTHER TELLS YOU HOW

TO MAKE A "NAME-BROOCH"

MOTHER, GRANNIE HAS AN OLD SILVER BROOCH WITH HER NAME ON IT. I'D LOVE TO HAVE A "NAME-BROOCH".

I'LL SHOW YOU HOW TO MAKE AN EMBROIDERED ONE IF YOU LIKE, JUDY!

YOU WILL NEED: A SMALL PIECE OF FINE EMBROIDERY CANVAS, A BROOCH FRAME, FILOSELLE EMBROIDERY SILK AND A SMALL LENGTH OF GOLD THREAD.

FIRST OF ALL, WRITE YOUR NAME NEATLY ON THE CANVAS WITH THIS BIRO, JUDY.

THEN, IRON THE INK DRY. WE'LL USE THE GOLD THREAD AND MATCHING SILK TO "COUCH" ALL ALONG YOUR NAME.

Judy

GOLD THREAD

MATCHING SILK

COUCHING

WHAT DO I DO TO THE BACKGROUND, MOTHER?

FILL IT IN WITH "TENT STITCH" USING TWO STRANDS OF SILK.

TENT STITCH

"TENT STITCH" IS WORKED LIKE THIS.

NOW FIX THE EMBROIDERY IN THE BROOCH FRAME.

IT'S LOVELY, JUDY.

DO YOU LIKE MY "NAME-BROOCH", JILL? I MADE IT MYSELF.

MOTHER TELLS YOU HOW

TO MAKE A NEEDLE ETCHING

I WOULD LIKE A PICTURE OF GRANNIE'S COTTAGE FOR MY BEDROOM, MOTHER.

WHY NOT WORK ONE IN NEEDLE ETCHING FROM THE PHOTOGRAPH YOU TOOK? WE'LL HAVE IT ENLARGED TO MEASURE EIGHT INCHES BY TEN INCHES.

MAKE A TRACING BY DRAWING THE OUTLINE OF THE PHOTOGRAPH ON TRANSPARENT PAPER LIKE THIS.

NOW TRACE YOUR PICTURE ON TO THE EMBROIDERY LINEN. USE CARBON PAPER AND A SHARP PENCIL.

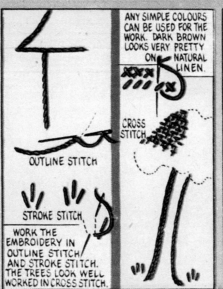

OUTLINE STITCH

STROKE STITCH

WORK THE EMBROIDERY IN OUTLINE STITCH AND STROKE STITCH. THE TREES LOOK WELL WORKED IN CROSS STITCH.

ANY SIMPLE COLOURS CAN BE USED FOR THE WORK. DARK BROWN LOOKS VERY PRETTY ON NATURAL LINEN.

CROSS STITCH

NOW THE EMBROIDERY IS FINISHED WE WILL MOUNT THE PICTURE ON STIFF CARDBOARD.

A NARROW GOLD OR DARK-COLOURED WOOD FRAME MAKES AN EFFECTIVE FINISH.

JILL, WHAT DO YOU THINK OF MY NEEDLE ETCHING?

IT'S LOVELY, JUDY. I'LL MAKE ONE TOO.

3

MOTHER ON NEEDLEWORK

MOTHER TELLS YOU HOW

TO DO DAISY WORK

GRANNY HAS SUCH A PRETTY SHAWL MADE OF WOOLLY DAISIES.

IT IS MADE IN "DAISY WORK", JUDY, I'LL SHOW YOU HOW TO DO IT, IF YOU LIKE.

YOU WILL NEED :—
ODDMENTS OF WOOL • A DISC OF THICK CARDBOARD, 2" IN DIAMETER • 12 PINS • A WOOL NEEDLE.

CARDBOARD
2" DIAMETER
DISC

MARK OUT THE PLACES FOR THE PINS, JUDY, THEN PUSH THEM IN THE THICKNESS OF THE CARDBOARD.

PINS IN DISC.

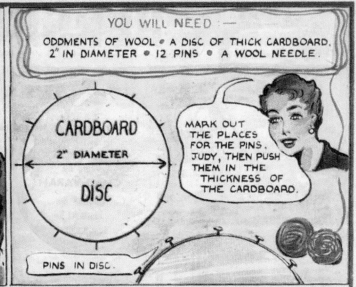

WIND THE THREE THICKNESSES OF WOOL OVER AND OVER THE PINS LIKE THIS.

CUT THE WOOL, LEAVING ABOUT 12 INCHES. THREAD IT INTO YOUR NEEDLE AND THEN OVERSEW THE CENTRE OF THE DAISY SO THAT THE LOOPS ARE SECURE.

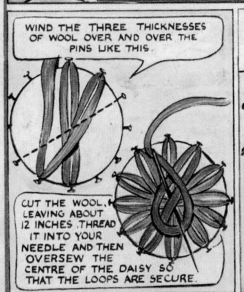

NOW FINISH THE CENTRE BY BACK-STITCHING ALL ROUND WITH ONE THREAD OF WOOL.

FINISH DAISY AND REMOVE DISC.

THAT'S RIGHT, JUDY, NOW WE'LL JOIN THE DAISIES TO MAKE A "FASCINATOR".

CROCHET EDGE TO DAISY —

ARRANGE THE DAISIES LIKE THIS AND JOIN NEATLY TOGETHER BY CROCHETING THROUGH THE LOOPS.

JOIN DAISIES.

OH, JUDY, HOW PRETTY YOUR SCARF LOOKS!

50

MOTHER TELLS YOU HOW

TO CROCHET

MUMMY, I DO WANT TO MAKE A CROCHET CAP LIKE JILL'S!

YOU'LL HAVE TO LEARN HOW TO CROCHET FIRST, JUDY, BUT IT'S VERY EASY.

FIRST MAKE A SLIP KNOT AND PUT THE HOOK INTO IT, THEN PASS THE HOOK ROUND THE THREAD AND PULL A LOOP THROUGH. THIS IS A CHAIN STITCH.

A. MAKE A SLIP KNOT LIKE THIS.

B. YOUR CHAIN SHOULD LOOK LIKE THIS.

NOW YOU MUST LEARN TO DO DOUBLE CROCHET, JUDY—THAT'S THE STITCH USED FOR JILL'S CAP.

PUT THE HOOK INTO THE CHAIN STITCH, PASS IT UNDER THE THREAD AND PULL A LOOP THROUGH (SEE DIAGRAM). PUT THE HOOK AGAIN UNDER THE THREAD AND PULL A LOOP THROUGH BOTH LOOPS.

TREBLE IS JUST LIKE DOUBLE CROCHET WITH AN EXTRA LOOP.

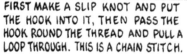

THE HOOK IS FIRST PASSED UNDER THE THREAD, THEN PUT INTO THE CHAIN STITCH AND A LOOP PULLED THROUGH (SEE DIAGRAM). THIS MAKES THREE LOOPS ON THE HOOK. PASS THE HOOK UNDER THE THREAD, PULL A LOOP THROUGH THE FIRST TWO LOOPS. REPEAT FOR THE LAST TWO LOOPS—THE ONE YOU HAVE PULLED THROUGH AND THE ONE ON THE HOOK.

WHEN YOU HAVE PRACTISED THESE THREE STITCHES AND CAN WORK THEM PERFECTLY EVENLY, YOU'LL BE ABLE TO CROCHET ANYTHING YOU LIKE, JUDY.

CHOOSE A GOOD PATTERN, FOLLOW THE INSTRUCTIONS CAREFULLY AND YOU CAN'T GO WRONG.

MOTHER TELLS YOU HOW

To Smock

JILL'S LITTLE SISTER HAS A LOVELY SMOCKED DRESS. I WOULD LIKE TO BE ABLE TO SMOCK, MOTHER.

I'LL SHOW YOU HOW TO SMOCK A SKIRT, JUDY.

CHOOSE CHECK MATERIAL FOR YOUR FIRST ATTEMPT, JUDY — THE SQUARES HELP YOU TO GATHER EVENLY.

HEM TOP OF SKIRT

JOIN

ALLOW THREE TIMES YOUR NORMAL SKIRT WIDTH AND JOIN THE MATERIAL TOGETHER IN ONE STRIP.

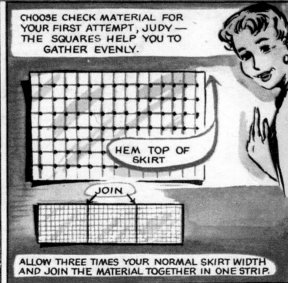

NOW GATHER, USING THE CHECKS AS A GUIDE. MAKE SIX ROWS OF GATHERS.

A THREAD FOR EACH ROW

PINS

PULL UP THE THREADS AND WIND THE COTTON ROUND PINS.

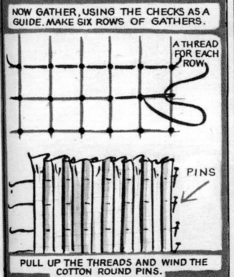

NOW FOR THE ACTUAL SMOCKING, JUDY.

WORK A ROW OF STEM STITCH TO MAKE *ROPE PATTERN*. EACH STITCH TAKES UP ONE PLEAT.

THEN WORK A ROW OF *CHEVRON STITCH*, FOLLOWING DIRECTION OF THE RED ARROW.

TO COMPLETE A DIAMOND WORK LIKE THIS.

WORK CHEVRON STITCH TO COMPLETE THREE ROWS OF DIAMONDS, THEN FINALLY A ROW OF ROPE PATTERN.

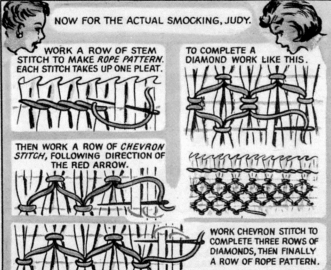

OH, WHAT A LOVELY SKIRT, JUDY!

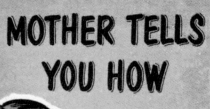

MOTHER TELLS YOU HOW

TO DO PATCHWORK

WHAT CAN I DO WITH ALL THESE OLD PIECES OF COTTON MATERIAL, MOTHER?

WHY NOT MAKE A PATCHWORK CUSHION COVER, JUDY.

BEGIN BY MAKING A CARDBOARD PATTERN THE SAME SHAPE AND SIZE AS THE ONE BELOW. IT MUST BE VERY ACCURATE OR THE PIECES YOU CUT FROM IT WON'T FIT TOGETHER.

USE THIS AS A PATTERN FOR THE CARDBOARD SHAPE.

NOW CUT PIECES OF STIFF PAPER INTO EXACTLY THE SAME SHAPE AND SIZE AS THE CARDBOARD. THIS IS A CHANCE TO GET RID OF OLD LETTERS AND ENVELOPES!

CUT THE PATCHES OF MATERIAL ¼ INCH LARGER THAN THE PIECES OF PAPER, THEN PRESS THE PATCHES FLAT.

TACK THE MATERIAL NEATLY OVER THE PAPER PATTERNS.

THERE, MOTHER — I'VE CUT AND TACKED SIXTY PATCHES!

GOOD. NOW YOU CAN BEGIN TO MAKE YOUR CUSHION COVER.

OVERSEW ALONG THE EDGES IN PAIRS LIKE THIS, FITTING THE SHAPES INTO EACH OTHER AND USING PLAIN TO ENCIRCLE PATTERNED ONES.

TAKE OUT THE TACKINGS (AND THE PAPER, IF YOU WISH).

THIS LOOKS SO PRETTY I THINK I'LL MAKE A PATCHWORK BED-SPREAD, MOTHER!

FIT IN TRIANGLES ALONG THE TOP AND BOTTOM, AND HALF PIECES ALONG THE SIDES. THIS MAKES THE SQUARE COMPLETE. WORK THE BACK IN THE SAME WAY.

MOTHER TELLS YOU HOW

TO MAKE

A STIFF PETTICOAT

LOOK, MOTHER, DON'T YOU THINK MY DRESS IS A BIT FLOPPY?

YES, JUDY, IT NEEDS A REALLY STIFF PETTICOAT UNDERNEATH.

VILENE IS A SPECIAL UNCRUSHABLE AND WASHABLE MATERIAL WHICH IS PERFECT FOR THE JOB

YOU WILL NEED 3 AND 3/4 YARDS FOR YOUR PETTICOAT, AND I'LL SHOW YOU HOW TO CUT IT OUT.

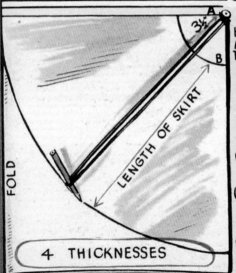

A
3½
B
LENGTH OF SKIRT
FOLD
4 THICKNESSES

FOLD THE MATERIAL IN HALF AND THEN IN HALF AGAIN, LAY IT OUT AND PIN THE FOUR THICKNESSES TOGETHER. MEASURE YOUR WAIST AND LENGTH. MAKE A STRING LOOP 3½ INCHES LONG AND FIX A DRAWING PIN IN THE CORNER (A). DRAW A QUARTER-CIRCLE FOR THE WAIST AS YOU SEE IN THE DIAGRAM, (B). MAKE A LOOP THE LENGTH YOU WANT THE SKIRT AND MARK OUT THE HEM IN THE SAME WAY, BUT REMEMBER TO ALLOW AN EXTRA 3½" FOR THE DISTANCE BETWEEN (A) AND (B).

NOW CUT ALONG THE CHALKED LINES - YOU CAN USE MY PINKING SHEARS FOR THE HEM.

PLACKET
8"

SEW THE SIDE SEAM LEAVING AN 8 INCH PLACKET OPENING. BIND THE WAIST WITH BIAS BINDING AND FASTEN WITH A HOOK AND EYE.

THERE, JUDY, THAT'S MUCH BETTER! A STIFF PETTICOAT JUST MAKES A SUMMER DRESS.

MOTHER TELLS YOU HOW

TO BRING A **PARTY DRESS** UP-TO-DATE

I *WOULD* LIKE A NEW DRESS FOR THE CHRISTMAS PARTIES, MOTHER.

I THINK WE COULD DO WONDERS WITH YOUR LAST YEAR'S ONE. TRY IT ON FOR SIZE, JUDY. IT'S QUITE FRESH FROM THE CLEANERS.

IT *DOES* LOOK BABYISH... BUT NEVER MIND, WE'LL SOON ALTER THAT.

FIRST OF ALL TAKE OUT THE SLEEVES AND THEN LET OUT THE BODICE IF IT'S A BIT TIGHT. LENGTHEN THE SKIRT BY ADDING A FRILL OF STIFF NET ALL ROUND THE HEM.

NOW WE'LL MAKE A VERY FULL OVERSKIRT OF NET.

NET IS NOT VERY EXPENSIVE, SO USE FOUR FULL WIDTHS. GATHER THE TOP EDGE INTO A RIBBON WAISTBAND AND MAKE A TINY SINGLE HEM ROUND THE BOTTOM.

THAT LOOKS BETTER! NOW WE'LL CUT OUT THE NECK AND ADD A YOKE AND FRILL OF NET TO MATCH THE SKIRT.

USE THE NET DOUBLE FOR THE YOKE AND THE FRILL. SEW BOWS OF NARROW SATIN RIBBON ALONG THE YOKE AND ALL OVER THE SKIRT.

I AM PLEASED, JUDY — THE DRESS LOOKS JUST LIKE A NEW ONE!

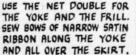

MOTHER TELLS YOU HOW

TO LENGTHEN A DRESS

WHY, JUDY... IT NEEDS LETTING DOWN AT LEAST FOUR INCHES!

JUDY'S COTTON FROCK IS TOO SHORT IN THE BODICE AS WELL AS IN THE SKIRT, SO BOTH MUST BE LENGTHENED.

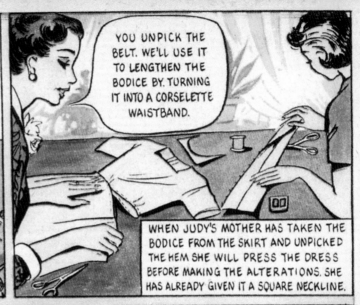

YOU UNPICK THE BELT. WE'LL USE IT TO LENGTHEN THE BODICE BY. TURNING IT INTO A CORSELETTE WAISTBAND.

WHEN JUDY'S MOTHER HAS TAKEN THE BODICE FROM THE SKIRT AND UNPICKED THE HEM SHE WILL PRESS THE DRESS BEFORE MAKING THE ALTERATIONS. SHE HAS ALREADY GIVEN IT A SQUARE NECKLINE.

THE HIGH WAISTED EFFECT OF THE CORSELETTE IS VERY PRETTY. WE'LL PUT A ZIP FASTENER INTO THE SIDE SEAM FOR A NEAT FIT.

FACE UP THE BOTTOM OF THE SKIRT WITH ANY COTTON MATERIAL TO MAKE A DEEP FALSE HEM.

I'VE FOUND THIS GAY SWISS TRIMMING. IT WILL BE JUST THE THING TO BRIGHTEN UP YOUR DRESS.

SWISS EMBROIDERED TRIMMING IS MADE IN BRIGHT FLOWER PATTERNS EMBROIDERED ON A WHITE OR NATURAL GROUND. IT'S QUITE INEXPENSIVE TO BUY.

OUTLINE THE NECK, CUFFS AND HEM WITH THE EMBROIDERY AND MAKE A BELT BY BACKING THE EMBROIDERY WITH PETERSHAM RIBBON. THE RESULT — A NEW DRESS!

MOTHER TELLS YOU HOW

TO FIT A DRESS

OH, MOTHER! THE BODICE OF THIS DRESS I'M MAKING IS MUCH TOO BIG.

NEVER MIND, JUDY. I'LL PIN IT SO THAT YOU CAN ALTER IT.

DARTS WILL GET RID OF THE BULGE AT THE WAISTLINE.

CENTRE BACK

CENTRE

BULGING

FITTING SMOOTHLY

MANY PEOPLE HAVE NARROW BACKS AND FIND PAPER PATTERNS TOO WIDE HERE.

THAT'S MUCH BETTER, JUDY. NOW WE'LL TACKLE THE BACK OF THE NECK.

FOUR TAPERING DARTS WILL MAKE THE DRESS FIT NEATLY HERE.

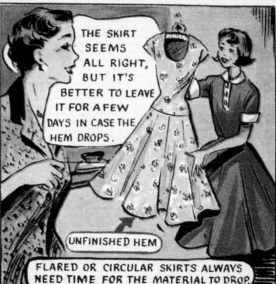

THE SKIRT SEEMS ALL RIGHT, BUT IT'S BETTER TO LEAVE IT FOR A FEW DAYS IN CASE THE HEM DROPS.

UNFINISHED HEM

FLARED OR CIRCULAR SKIRTS ALWAYS NEED TIME FOR THE MATERIAL TO DROP.

OH, JUDY, WHAT A LOVELY DRESS! WHERE DID YOU GET IT?

I MADE IT MYSELF— MOTHER HELPED ME TO FIT IT PROPERLY.

MOTHER TELLS YOU HOW

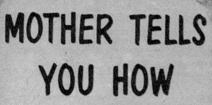

TO MAKE A SUMMER BLOUSE

I'VE NO BLOUSE TO WEAR WITH THIS COTTON SKIRT, MOTHER.

COME SHOPPING WITH ME AND I'LL SHOW YOU HOW TO MAKE ONE FOR UNDER FOUR SHILLINGS.

THESE CHECK HANDKERCHIEFS WILL MAKE AN ATTRACTIVE BLOUSE, JUDY. YOU'LL NEED TWO LARGE ONES.

1/11

COTTON HANDKERCHIEFS CAN BE BOUGHT IN LOVELY COLOURS FOR ABOUT 1/11d. EACH. TWO SQUARES—EACH 27" BY 27"—WILL FIT ANY SIZE.

27"

CUT EACH SQUARE IN HALF DIAGONALLY AND HEM THE RAW EDGES NEATLY.

DARTS

SHAPE FOR UNDERARM

SHAPE FOR UNDERARM

TACK UP AS SHOWN HERE AND THEN TRY ON. YOU MAY HAVE TO ADJUST THE DARTS TO FIT YOU. NOW SEW FIRMLY ON THE WRONG SIDE, CUTTING AWAY THE SURPLUS MATERIAL.

THE SHOULDER TIES MAKE THE BLOUSE FIT NEATLY.

TIE THE FOUR PAIRS OF POINTS INTO BOWS AT THE WAIST AND ON THE SHOULDER, AS SHOWN.

YOU DO HAVE SMASHING CLOTHES, JUDY!

MOTHER TELLS YOU HOW

TO MAKE PIN-CUSHIONS

PIN-CUSHIONS MAY BE OLD-FASHIONED, MOTHER, BUT THEY'RE JOLLY USEFUL!

YES, JUDY, AND THEY MAKE GOOD INEXPENSIVE CHRISTMAS PRESENTS TOO. I'LL SHOW YOU HOW GRANNIE USED TO MAKE HERS.

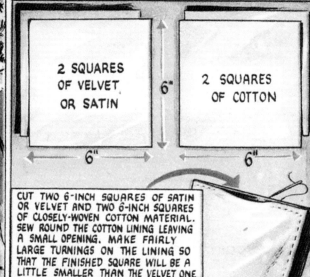

2 SQUARES OF VELVET OR SATIN

6"

2 SQUARES OF COTTON

6"   6"

CUT TWO 6-INCH SQUARES OF SATIN OR VELVET AND TWO 6-INCH SQUARES OF CLOSELY-WOVEN COTTON MATERIAL. SEW ROUND THE COTTON LINING LEAVING A SMALL OPENING. MAKE FAIRLY LARGE TURNINGS ON THE LINING SO THAT THE FINISHED SQUARE WILL BE A LITTLE SMALLER THAN THE VELVET ONE.

NOW FOR THE SECRET — FILL THE COTTON LINING WITH DRIED COFFEE GROUNDS!

THE COFFEE GROUNDS STUFFING PREVENTS NEEDLES OR PINS FROM RUSTING IN THE CUSHION.

ON THE WRONG SIDE, SEW ROUND THREE SIDES OF THE VELVET COVER AND THEN TURN IT INSIDE OUT. SEW UP THE OPENING IN THE CUSHION SECURELY AND THEN SLIP IT INTO THE COVER. FASTEN THE COVER AND ADD A FRILL OF RIBBON OR LACE ALL ROUND THE EDGE.

SATIN COVER

HANDY PIN-CUSHIONS FOR DRESS-MAKING ARE MADE IN THE SAME WAY, BUT ARE QUITE TINY. A TWO-INCH SQUARE IS BIG ENOUGH. SEW A LOOP TO ONE CORNER FOR A SAFETY PIN SO THAT YOU CAN ATTACH THE PIN-CUSHION TO YOUR DRESS.

OR

MAKE A WRIST BAND OF ELASTIC AND SEW IT TO THE BACK OF THE CUSHION.

I LOVE YOUR WRIST PIN-CUSHION, JUDY! I WISH YOU'D MAKE ONE FOR ME TOO.

MOTHER TELLS YOU HOW

TO SEW UP YOUR KNITTING

I'VE FINISHED KNITTING MY JERSEY, MOTHER. HOW SHALL I SEW IT UP?

THE SEAMS MUST BE ELASTIC, JUDY—THAT IS WHY I TOLD YOU TO BE CAREFUL ABOUT THE EDGE STITCH.

ALWAYS WORK ONE KNIT STITCH AT THE BEGINNING OF EACH ROW.

FIRM EDGE FOR A NEAT SEAM.

YOU CAN'T EXPECT A NEAT SEAM, UNLESS YOU HAVE A NEAT EDGE.

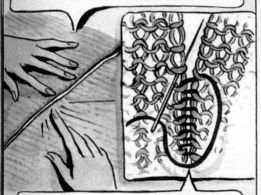

NOW HOLD THE TWO EDGES TOGETHER LIKE THIS.

LINK THE SEAMS TOGETHER BY SEWING THE EDGE STITCHES IN PAIRS.

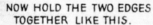

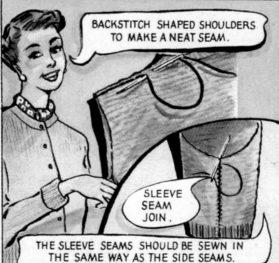

BACKSTITCH SHAPED SHOULDERS TO MAKE A NEAT SEAM.

SLEEVE SEAM JOIN.

THE SLEEVE SEAMS SHOULD BE SEWN IN THE SAME WAY AS THE SIDE SEAMS.

OH, JUDY, WHAT A LOVELY JUMPER.

MOTHER TELLS YOU HOW

TO MAKE A SCARF JERKIN

I WOULD SO LIKE A JERKIN LIKE THIS ONE, MOTHER.

THEN HERE'S YOUR CHANCE TO USE THAT BIG SCARF WHICH CLASHES SO BADLY WITH YOUR COAT.

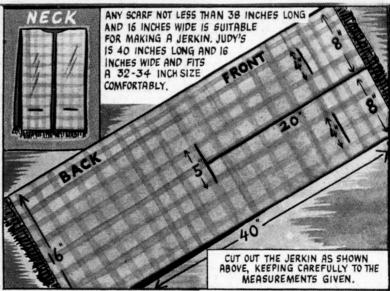

ANY SCARF NOT LESS THAN 38 INCHES LONG AND 16 INCHES WIDE IS SUITABLE FOR MAKING A JERKIN. JUDY'S IS 40 INCHES LONG AND 16 INCHES WIDE AND FITS A 32-34 INCH SIZE COMFORTABLY.

NECK

FRONT

BACK

8"

8"

4½"

4½"

20"

5"

16"

40"

CUT OUT THE JERKIN AS SHOWN ABOVE, KEEPING CAREFULLY TO THE MEASUREMENTS GIVEN.

NOW WORK DOUBLE CROCHET ALL ROUND THE CUT EDGES OF THE NECK AND FRONTS.

TURN OVER A NARROW HEM AND, WITH MATCHING WOOL AND A Nº 12 WOOL CROCHET HOOK, WORK AS SHOWN HERE.

HEM ROUND POCKET SLITS, THEN CUT TWO PIECES 4 x 4 INCHES FROM ANY SUITABLE MATERIAL AND SEW TO THE BACK OF POCKETS AS A LINING.

INSIDE SCARF

POCKET SLIT

4" POCKET LINING

4"

NOW TRY IT ON FOR FIT, JUDY, AND THEN WE'LL SEW THE SIDES TOGETHER AT THE WAIST.

SEW HERE

THE LITTLE REVERS CAN BE TACKED DOWN ON THE SHOULDER.

GOSH, JUDY, YOU DO LOOK GROWN-UP AND SMART!

AND IT'S JOLLY WARM TOO.

MOTHER TELLS YOU HOW

TO MAKE A BURMESE SKIRT

WHEN WE'RE AWAY, MOTHER, I WOULD LIKE SOMETHING TO WEAR OVER MY SWIMSUIT TO GO FROM THE HOUSE TO THE BEACH.

I'LL SHOW YOU HOW TO MAKE A BURMESE SKIRT, JUDY. YOU CAN USE IT AS A SUN-BATHING MAT AS WELL.

TOWELLING

I THINK THIS IS THE PRETTIEST TOWELLING, JUDY.

FINISHED SEAM

BUY 2 YARDS OF BRIGHT-COLOURED TOWELLING AND JOIN THE ENDS TOGETHER TO MAKE A TUBE.

THAT'S RIGHT, JUDY. NOW PUT IT ON AND HOLD IT WITH YOUR HANDS CROSSED.

MAKE A BIG FOLD FROM SIDE TO SIDE. HOLD IT TIGHT ROUND YOUR WAIST AND TUCK IT IN.

IT'S VERY COMFORTABLE, AND THERE'S PLENTY OF ROOM FOR WALKING.

YES, AND YOU CAN WEAR IT UP HIGH, IF YOU LIKE, TO MAKE IT A DRESS.

USE YOUR SKIRT AS A TOWEL AFTER SWIMMING, AND THEN YOU CAN SPREAD IT OUT AS A MAT FOR SUN-BATHING.

MOTHER TELLS YOU HOW

TO MAKE A **SHORTIE NIGHTIE**

MOTHER, I DO NEED A NEW NIGHTDRESS.

YES, YOU DO, JUDY. WHY DON'T YOU MAKE YOURSELF A 'SHORTIE'?

YOU NEED 2½ YARDS DRIP-DRY COTTON, AND 4 YARDS OF LACE.

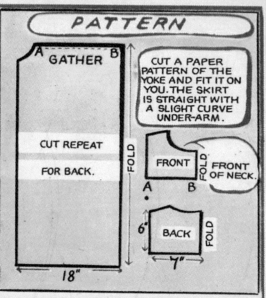

PATTERN

A — B
GATHER

CUT REPEAT FOR BACK.

FOLD

18"

CUT A PAPER PATTERN OF THE YOKE AND FIT IT ON YOU. THE SKIRT IS STRAIGHT WITH A SLIGHT CURVE UNDER-ARM.

FRONT — FOLD — FRONT OF NECK.

A — B

6" BACK FOLD

7"

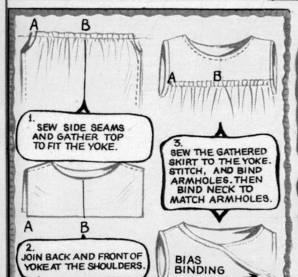

A — B

A — B

1. SEW SIDE SEAMS AND GATHER TOP TO FIT THE YOKE.

A — B

2. JOIN BACK AND FRONT OF YOKE AT THE SHOULDERS.

3. SEW THE GATHERED SKIRT TO THE YOKE. STITCH, AND BIND ARMHOLES. THEN BIND NECK TO MATCH ARMHOLES.

BIAS BINDING

NOW YOU MUST TRIM THE HEM AND THE YOKE WITH LACE, JUDY.

GATHER LACE AND SEW ROUND HEM AND YOKE.

OH, JUDY, I MUST MAKE A NIGHTIE LIKE YOURS!

MOTHER TELLS YOU HOW

TO MAKE A "SCOTTIE" NIGHTDRESS CASE

I REALLY NEED A NEW NIGHTDRESS CASE, MOTHER, BUT I'D LIKE IT TO BE A DOLL OR SOMETHING THIS TIME.

A "SCOTTIE" CASE WOULD LOOK WELL ON YOUR DIVAN COVER, JUDY.

CUT A PAPER PATTERN TO SCALE FROM THE DIAGRAM. THE DOUBLE LINE INDICATES THE TURNING.

LEAVE OPEN FOR ZIPPER

EACH SQUARE = 1 INCH

BLACK VELVET OR FUR FABRIC IS THE BEST MATERIAL TO USE. LOOK OUT FOR A ½ YARD REMNANT.

PIN THE PATTERN TO THE MATERIAL AND CUT OUT CAREFULLY.

VELVET OR FUR FABRIC

SATIN

USE A REMNANT OF SATIN FOR THE LINING AND THE BACK OF THE CASE. CUT BOTH THESE FROM YOUR PATTERN.

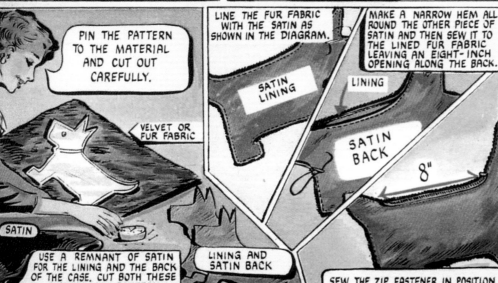

LINE THE FUR FABRIC WITH THE SATIN AS SHOWN IN THE DIAGRAM.

SATIN LINING

LINING AND SATIN BACK

MAKE A NARROW HEM ALL ROUND THE OTHER PIECE OF SATIN AND THEN SEW IT TO THE LINED FUR FABRIC LEAVING AN EIGHT-INCH OPENING ALONG THE BACK.

LINING

SATIN BACK

8"

SEW THE ZIP FASTENER IN POSITION

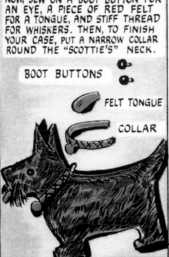

NOW, SEW ON A BOOT BUTTON FOR AN EYE, A PIECE OF RED FELT FOR A TONGUE, AND STIFF THREAD FOR WHISKERS. THEN, TO FINISH YOUR CASE, PUT A NARROW COLLAR ROUND THE "SCOTTIE'S" NECK.

BOOT BUTTONS

FELT TONGUE

COLLAR

WHAT A LOVELY "SCOTTIE", JUDY!

I'M GLAD YOU LIKE IT, JILL! IT'S MY NEW NIGHT-DRESS CASE.

MOTHER TELLS YOU HOW

TO MAKE A SPORTS HAT

MOTHER, I WOULD LIKE A NEW HAT FOR OUR RAMBLING CLUB'S FIRST OUTING.

YOU CAN SOON MAKE ONE, JUDY. YOU CAN USE THE PIECE OF JERSEY CLOTH LEFT OVER FROM YOUR SKIRT.

YOU WILL NEED:— A PIECE OF JERSEY CLOTH, 9 INCHES LONG AND 10 INCHES WIDE. 1 OZ OF DOUBLE-KNITTING WOOL IN A MATCHING OR CONTRASTING COLOUR (YOU COULD USE UP ODDMENTS FOR A MULTICOLOURED EFFECT). A No. 3 CROCHET HOOK. AN ALICE BAND.

9"

10"

DOUBLE-KNITTING WOOL

ALICE BAND

A No. 3 CROCHET HOOK

MAKE A ROLLED HEM ALONG ONE LONG SIDE AND THE TWO SHORT SIDES OF THE JERSEY CLOTH. THEN MAKE A HEM ½ INCH WIDE FOR THE ALICE BAND ALONG THE LAST SIDE.

HEM FOR THE ALICE BAND

FOLD THE CLOTH IN HALF. WORK CROCHET LOOPS OF 5 CHAIN, 1 DOUBLE CROCHET ALONG THE EDGE, AND THEN ROUND AND ROUND FOR 5 OR 6 INS.

DRAW UP THE END, JUDY, AND SEW ON A GOOD FAT TASSEL. NOW PUT IN THE ALICE BAND.

INSERT ALICE BAND

GATHER THE END

USE WOOL LIKE THIS TO MAKE A TASSEL

OH, JUDY, WHAT A WONDERFUL HAT!

MOTHER TELLS YOU HOW

TO MAKE A
Stocking Cap

MOTHER, WHAT CAN I DO WITH THESE ODD BALLS OF WOOL?

THEY WOULD MAKE A SPLENDID STOCKING CAP, DEAR.

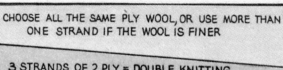

CHOOSE ALL THE SAME PLY WOOL, OR USE MORE THAN ONE STRAND IF THE WOOL IS FINER

3 STRANDS OF 2 PLY = DOUBLE KNITTING.
2 STRANDS OF 2 PLY = 4 PLY.

WITH Nº 8 NEEDLES, CAST ON 98 STITCHES AND WORK IN KNIT 2, PURL 2 RIB ALL THE TIME. USE THE DIFFERENT COLOURS IN BROAD STRIPES, 2 TO 3 INCHES WIDE.

HOW MUCH MORE SHALL I KNIT, MOTHER?

ABOUT ANOTHER TEN INCHES, DEAR. A FAIRLY LONG CAP WILL LOOK BEST OVER YOUR SHORT HAIR.

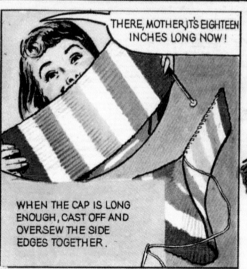

THERE, MOTHER, IT'S EIGHTEEN INCHES LONG NOW!

WHEN THE CAP IS LONG ENOUGH, CAST OFF AND OVERSEW THE SIDE EDGES TOGETHER.

NOW GATHER UP ONE END. FOR THE FINISHING TOUCH, MAKE A TASSEL ON A CHAIN AND SEW IT IN THE MIDDLE.

OH, WHAT A SMASHING CAP!

67

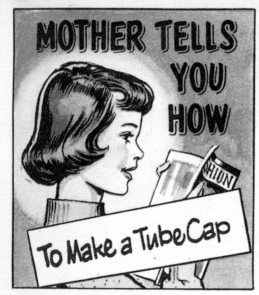

MOTHER TELLS YOU HOW

To Make a Tube Cap

MOTHER, DO YOU THINK I COULD MAKE ONE OF THESE CAPS?

OF COURSE YOU CAN, JUDY.

YOU WILL NEED:

6oz DOUBLE KNITTING WOOL AND 2 No.6 KNITTING NEEDLES, PLEASE.

CAST ON 88 sts. AND WORK IN KNIT 1, PURL 1 RIB.

THERE, MOTHER. HOW MUCH MUST I DO?

AT LEAST 18 INCHES, JUDY.

CAST OFF, SEW UP THE LONG EDGES AND YOUR CAP IS FINISHED.

GOSH, THAT LOOKS WARM, JUDY!

MOTHER TELLS YOU HOW

TO MAKE AN EASTER BONNET

I WOULD LIKE A WHITE HAT FOR EASTER, MOTHER, TO MATCH MY WHITE GLOVES.

YOU CAN MAKE ONE YOURSELF VERY EASILY AND QUICKLY, JUDY. I'LL HELP YOU.

YOU WILL NEED HALF A YARD OF RAYON JERSEY AND A NO. 6 CROCHET HOOK.

CUT LIKE THIS

8"

8"

½" WIDE STRIPS

18"

CUT THE MATERIAL INTO CROSS-WAY STRIPS, JUDY, TWO OF THEM EIGHT INCHES WIDE AND ALL THE REST HALF AN INCH WIDE.

JOIN THE NARROW STRIPS TOGETHER THEN WIND THEM INTO A BALL.

NOW BEGIN TO WORK THE CROWN OF THE BONNET BY MAKING A CIRCLE OF 6 CHAINS JOINED WITH A SINGLE CROCHET.

WORK IN MESH PATTERN (1 TREBLE CROCHET, 3 CHAINS) 6 TIMES INTO THIS CIRCLE. THEN CONTINUE ROUND FOR A FURTHER 3 ROWS OF MESH, WORKING AN EXTRA CHAIN IN THE MESH PATTERN IN EACH ROW. NOW WORK 3 MORE ROWS OF MESH USING 6 CHAINS FOR THE LOOPS.

THAT'S RIGHT, JUDY. THE CAP SHOULD MEASURE ABOUT SIX INCHES DEEP.

NOW, MAKE EACH WIDE STRIP INTO A DOUBLE BAND USING THE WRONG SIDE OF THE MATERIAL. SEW ONE BAND ROUND THE CROCHET CROWN AND MAKE THE OTHER INTO A BOW. FINALLY, SEW THE BOW AT THE BACK OF THE HAT.

SEW BAND TO CROCHET CROWN

4"

JOIN FOR BOW

OH, JUDY, YOU DO LOOK SMART!

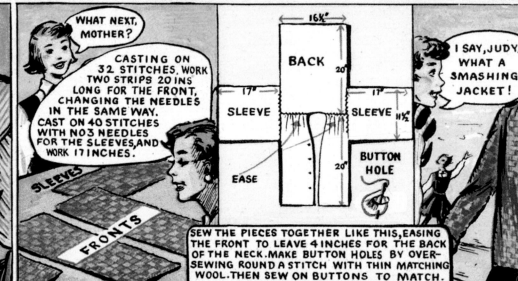

MOTHER TELLS YOU HOW

TO MAKE A COLLEGE SCARF

WE ALL WANT TO KNIT OURSELVES COLLEGE SCARVES, MOTHER. COULD YOU SHOW US HOW?

YES, OF COURSE, JUDY. YOU CAN MAKE THEM IN A VERY SIMPLE RIB PATTERN.

FOR A SCARF 2 YARDS LONG BY 18 INCHES WIDE, YOU WILL NEED: 11 OZS OF SPORTS WOOL IN TWO COLOURS (22 OZS IN ALL) AND 1 PAIR OF NO. 7 NEEDLES.

CAST ON 126 STITCHES VERY LOOSELY, JUDY.

PATTERN (ALL ROWS ALIKE)—ONE STITCH PLAIN, ONE STITCH PURL ALL ALONG THE ROW. WORK 4 INCHES IN EACH COLOUR.

NOW IT'S ONLY A MATTER OF TIME! SEE HOW QUICK YOU CAN BE, JUDY!

THERE, MOTHER! IT'S TWO YARDS LONG AT LAST!

GOOD! NOW CAST OFF LOOSELY, AND MAKE THE FRINGE.

FRINGE

CUT THE WOOL INTO 6" LENGTHS AND HOOK IT THROUGH AS SHOWN HERE.

I SAY, JUDY, THAT'S A FINE COLLEGE SCARF YOU'RE WEARING!

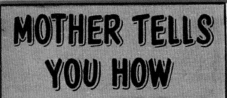

MOTHER TELLS YOU HOW

TO MAKE A BUCKET-BAG

MOTHER, COULD I DO ANYTHING WITH THIS PIECE OF MATERIAL LEFT OVER FROM MY DRESS?

YOU'LL NEED A BEACH-BAG OF SOME KIND, JUDY, SO LET'S USE IT TO MAKE A BUCKET-BAG.

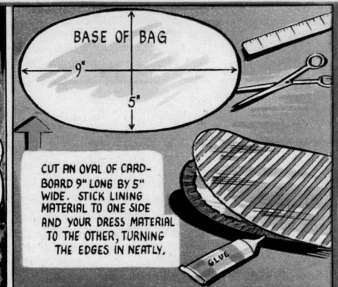

BASE OF BAG

9"

5"

CUT AN OVAL OF CARD-BOARD 9" LONG BY 5" WIDE. STICK LINING MATERIAL TO ONE SIDE AND YOUR DRESS MATERIAL TO THE OTHER, TURNING THE EDGES IN NEATLY.

GLUE

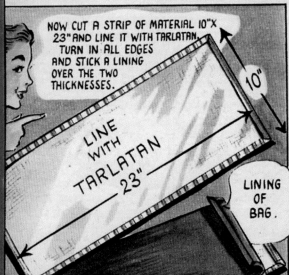

NOW CUT A STRIP OF MATERIAL 10" X 23" AND LINE IT WITH TARLATAN. TURN IN ALL EDGES AND STICK A LINING OVER THE TWO THICKNESSES.

10"

LINE WITH TARLATAN — 23"

LINING OF BAG.

MACHINE A DOUBLE STRIP OF BRAID TO EACH SIDE OF THE BAG TO MAKE A HANDLE LIKE THIS. NOW JOIN THE SIDE, SEWING THE BRAID OVER THE JOIN.

BRAID OVER JOIN.

JOIN THE BASE TO THE TOP BY OVERSEWING ALL THE EDGES TOGETHER. COVER THE STITCHING BY STICKING ON NARROW BRAID TO MATCH THE HANDLES.

BRAID OVER STITCHING.

OH, JUDY, HOW DID YOU GET A BAG TO MATCH YOUR DRESS?

MOTHER TOLD ME HOW TO MAKE ONE!

4

MOTHER'S SUPER RECIPE IDEAS

MOTHER TELLS YOU HOW

TO COOK SUMMER VEGETABLES

GREENS SHOULD BE COOKED AS SOON AS POSSIBLE AFTER THEY ARE CUT, JUDY.

WASH THEM, THEN SHRED THEM FINELY. PUT INTO A SAUCEPAN WITH 1 OR 2 CUPS OF BOILING WATER AND BOIL WITH THE LID TIGHTLY SHUT FOR 10 OR 15 MINUTES. DRAIN AND SERVE WITH KNOBS OF BUTTER.

SPINACH NEEDS NO WATER TO COOK IT IN. WASH WELL, PUT IT INTO A SAUCEPAN AND BOIL FOR TEN MINUTES. SERVE AS FOR GREENS.

SAVE THE PEA PODS, JUDY. BOILED THEY WILL MAKE VERY GOOD FRESH PEA SOUP.

CHOOSE SMALL YOUNG PEAS, SHELL THEM AND COOK IN BOILING WATER TO COVER. ADD A LITTLE SUGAR AND A SPRIG OF MINT.

RUNNER BEANS NEED STRINGING EVEN WHEN THEY ARE YOUNG. TOP AND TAIL THEM LIKE THIS FIRST.

FRENCH BEANS NEED TOPPING AND TAILING TOO. USE ONLY WHEN YOUNG AND BREAK INTO SMALL LENGTHS. COOK BOTH RUNNER AND FRENCH BEANS IN BOILING WATER.

WHETHER YOU USE SALT OR NOT IS A PERSONAL MATTER. SOME PEOPLE HATE VEGETABLES COOKED WITHOUT IT AND SOME SAY IT RUINS THE NATURAL FLAVOUR. I LIKE A LITTLE PUT IN JUST BEFORE THE VEGETABLES ARE DONE.

THE GOLDEN RULES FOR SUCCESS, JUDY, ARE TO USE YOUNG VEGETABLES AND JUST ENOUGH WATER TO COOK THEM IN.

MOTHER TELLS YOU HOW

TO MAKE JELLIES

MOST PEOPLE LIKE JELLIES AND THEY ARE VERY EASY TO MAKE, JUDY. LET'S TRY A MILK ONE TODAY.

THE BEST FLAVOURS ARE COFFEE, CHOCOLATE OR VANILLA. SWEETEN TO TASTE AND MIX WITH ONE PINT OF MILK AS YOU WOULD FOR A HOT MILK DRINK, BUT RATHER STRONGER. THEN ADD GELATINE DISSOLVED IN A LITTLE HOT WATER (THE DIRECTIONS ON THE GELATINE PACKET WILL TELL YOU HOW MUCH TO USE TO SET ONE PINT OF LIQUID).

RINSE THE MOULD IN COLD WATER THEN POUR THE MIXTURE INTO IT. LEAVE IN A COOL PLACE UNTIL SET.

TO TAKE OUT, LOOSEN THE JELLY WITH A KNIFE ROUND THE EDGE OF THE MOULD.

PUT A DISH ON TOP, SHAKE AND TURN OVER. THE JELLY SHOULD COME OUT PERFECTLY.

FRUIT JELLIES LOOK SO PRETTY AND ARE USEFUL FOR USING UP ODD PIECES OF FRUIT.

Fruit Jellies

Cut the prepared fruit into small pieces – banana, apple, pear, pineapple, orange sections and whole red cherries are lovely with lemon jelly. Dissolve gelatine (same amount as for a pint of liquid) in ¼ pint of lemon squash or sweetened lemon juice. Make up with water or fruit juice to ¾ pint and wait until it begins to stiffen. Then add the fruit, which will remain distributed in the jelly instead of sinking to the bottom.

WHEN IT IS SET, LOOSEN THE EDGES WITH A KNIFE AND DIP IN HOT WATER. TURN OUT AS USUAL.

FATHER'S FAVOURITE IS A SAVOURY JELLY, SO WE'VE MADE CHICKEN ASPIC FOR LUNCH TODAY!

SAVOURY ASPIC JELLY CAN BE BOUGHT IN PACKETS. PUT HALF A HARD-BOILED EGG AT THE BOTTOM OF LITTLE MOULDS, ADD DICED COOKED CARROTS AND PEAS AND THE CUT UP CHICKEN PIECES. MAKE THE JELLY AS EXPLAINED ON THE PACKET AND POUR INTO THE MOULDS WHEN IT HAS COOLED A LITTLE. LEAVE TO SET, THEN TURN OUT AND TRIM WITH LETTUCE LEAVES AND SLICED TOMATOES.

MOTHER TELLS YOU HOW

TO MAKE SCOTCH PANCAKES

Scotch Pancakes

YOU WILL NEED :—

1 TEACUPFUL OF PLAIN FLOUR.

1 TEASPOONFUL OF CREAM OF TARTAR.

½ TEASPOONFUL BI-CARBONATE OF SODA.

1 EGG (BEATEN WELL).

MILK, TO MAKE ¾ PINT OF LIQUID WITH THE EGG.

1 DESSERTSPOONFUL SUGAR.

MOTHER TELLS YOU HOW

Baked Alaska

MOTHER, COULD I COOK SOMETHING SPECIAL FOR MY FRIENDS ON SATURDAY EVENING?

YES, IT'S SILLY TO KEEP TO SIMPLE THINGS ALL THE TIME. WE'LL MAKE A BAKED ALASKA.

You will need

1 ICE-CREAM BLOCK—MIXED OR PLAIN.
1 SPONGE CAKE—CUT TO SAME SIZE AS THE BLOCK.
2 EGG WHITES.
3 ozs. CASTOR SUGAR
A FEW WALNUTS AND GLACE CHERRIES.

ORGANISATION AND SPEED ARE THE ESSENTIALS FOR SUCCESS.

FIRST, SET THE OVEN TO REGULO NINE, WHILE I CUT THE CAKE TO FIT THE BLOCK.

NOW WHISK THE EGG WHITES WITH A PINCH OF SALT, UNTIL THEY ARE STIFF. NOW FOLD IN THE CASTOR SUGAR.

ARRANGE THE CAKE AND THE ICE-CREAM ON AN OVEN-PROOF DISH

HERE IS THE QUICK PART. COVER WITH THE MIXTURE AND DECORATE AS QUICKLY AS POSSIBLE. THE ICE-CREAM MUST BE COVERED COMPLETELY. NOW COOK FOR THREE MINUTES.

CHRIS GARVEY

OH, THIS IS LUSCIOUS!

MOTHER TELLS YOU HOW

TO PREPARE GRAPEFRUIT

ALWAYS CHOOSE FRUIT THAT IS HEAVY FOR ITS SIZE, JUDY.

THE KIND WITH A SPOTTED SKIN IS THE SWEETEST AND CAN USUALLY BE EATEN WITHOUT SUGAR.

TO PREPARE THEM FOR EATING, A PROPERLY CURVED GRAPEFRUIT KNIFE DOES THE JOB BEST.

ALLOW ONE GRAPEFRUIT FOR TWO PEOPLE. WIPE THE OUTSIDE WELL WITH A DAMP CLOTH AND, IF POSSIBLE, LEAVE OVERNIGHT IN A COLD LARDER OR FRIDGE.

AFTER DIVIDING THE FRUIT IN HALF. CUT ALL ROUND THE OUTER RIND, REMOVE ANY PIPS AND THEN SEPARATE EACH SEGMENT OF FRUIT AWAY FROM THE SKIN. EVERY SEGMENT SHOULD BE COMPLETE SO THAT IT CAN BE TAKEN OUT IN A SPOON LIKE THIS.

SPRINKLE WITH CASTOR SUGAR AND GARNISH WITH A CHERRY.

FOR A CHANGE, PUT THE GRAPEFRUIT HALVES READY SPRINKLED WITH SUGAR UNDER THE GRILL UNTIL THE SUGAR HAS BROWNED.

SERVE THE GRAPEFRUIT HALVES IN GLASS DISHES AND EAT WITH TEASPOONS OR SPECIAL GRAPEFRUIT SPOONS.

MOTHER TELLS YOU HOW

to Decorate Biscuits

JILL AND BOB ARE COMING ROUND TONIGHT, MOTHER. WHAT CAN I MAKE QUICKLY, TO EAT WITH OUR COCOA?

THERE ARE PLENTY OF BISCUITS, JUDY — WE'LL MAKE THEM LOOK GAY, WITH THIS.

PINK, WHITE AND CHOCOLATE ICING CAN BE BOUGHT IN TUBES, ALL READY TO USE.

SQUEEZE GENTLY, AND MAKE LITTLE CIRCLES, JUDY.

PUT A DAB IN THE CENTRE AND STICK A HALF WALNUT ON TOP.

ON THESE SHORTBREAD BISCUITS, WE'LL PUT AN EDGE-ING OF WHITE AND PINK ICING ALL ROUND.

NOW ARRANGE THE BISCUITS ON PLATES.

OH, JUDY, THESE ARE DELICIOUS!

MOTHER TELLS YOU HOW

TO GARNISH ⁕ FOOD ⁕

OH, MOTHER, THAT *DOES* MAKE ME FEEL HUNGRY.

IT'S ONLY A PLAIN GREEN SALAD, JUDY, BUT THE GARNISH MAKES IT LOOK EXCITING.

A FAMOUS CHEF ONCE SAID THAT ALL DISHES SHOULD BE GARNISHED IN AT LEAST FOUR COLOURS, SO FOR A LETTUCE SALAD USE SLICES OF HARD-BOILED EGGS, SPRIGS OF CELERY AND BEETROOT STRIPS — YELLOW, WHITE, PALE GREEN AND RED.

1. ONION SOUP — GARNISH WITH FRIED BREAD SQUARES TOPPED WITH FINE, CHOPPED PARSLEY.
2. MUSHROOM SOUP — GARNISH WITH A FEW NASTURTIUM PETALS.
3. TOMATO SOUP — GARNISH WITH DABS OF WHIPPED CREAM.
4. CLEAR SOUP — GARNISH WITH WAFER-THIN SLICES OF LEMON, OR GREEN PEAS AND TINY DISCS OF CARROTS.

ONION SOUP

MUSHROOM SOUP

CLEAR SOUP

TOMATO SOUP

THE HUMBLE HADDOCK LOOKS VERY RICH DRESSED UP LIKE THIS, DOESN'T IT, JUDY?

GARNISH STEAMED WHOLE FISH WITH CIRCLES OF CUCUMBER OUTLINED WITH QUARTERS OF TOMATO. PUT A BORAGE FLOWER IN THE CENTRE OF EACH CUCUMBER SLICE.

BORAGE

THERE, THAT'S THE END OF SUNDAY'S JOINT.

CUT RADISHES LIKE THIS AND CRISP THEM IN COLD WATER. THEY WILL THEN OPEN OUT INTO "FLOWERS".

ARRANGE SLICES OF MEAT ON A BED OF POTATO SALAD, SPRINKLED WITH CHOPPED CHIVES AND SIEVED HARD-BOILED EGG YOLKS. TRIM WITH WATERCRESS AND RADISHES CUT INTO "FLOWERS".

THANK YOU, JUDY. THAT EGG DOES LOOK GOOD.

SPRINKLE POACHED OR FRIED EGGS WITH A LITTLE PAPRIKA.

MOTHER TELLS YOU HOW

TO USE OLD CHEESE

MOTHER, I'M AFRAID I'VE LET THIS CHEESE GO DRY WHILE YOU WERE AWAY.

THAT'S ALL RIGHT, DEAR. WE'LL MAKE CHEESE STRAWS WITH IT.

YOU WILL NEED

FINELY GRATED CHEESE
*
STALE WHITE BREAD
*
MELTED BUTTER
*
CAYENNE PEPPER

STALE BREAD

MELTED BUTTER

GRATED CHEESE

SLICE THE BREAD ABOUT ¼ INCH THICK.

CUT OFF ALL THE CRUSTS

THEN CUT IT INTO 'STRAWS' 3 INCHES LONG, AND ¼ INCH WIDE.

YOU CAN ALSO CUT FANCY SHAPES WITH PASTRY CUTTERS.

DIP THE 'STRAWS' INTO THE BUTTER AND THEN TOSS IN THE CHEESE.

FINELY SPRINKLE WITH CAYENNE PEPPER.

HAVE THE OVEN AT 400°F OR REGULO 6, AND COOK UNTIL BROWN. SERVE WITH PARSLEY.

COME AND HAVE SOME HOT CHEESE SAVOURIES!

MOTHER TELLS YOU HOW

To Make Unusual Sandwiches

I'M SO TIRED OF ORDINARY SANDWICHES, MOTHER!

I'LL SHOW YOU HOW TO MAKE SOME UNUSUAL ONES, JUDY.

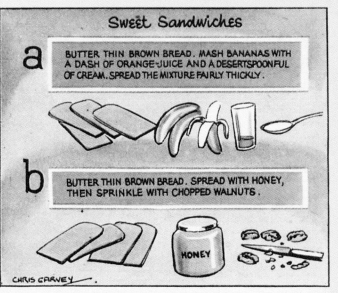

Sweet Sandwiches

a BUTTER THIN BROWN BREAD. MASH BANANAS WITH A DASH OF ORANGE-JUICE AND A DESERTSPOONFUL OF CREAM. SPREAD THE MIXTURE FAIRLY THICKLY.

b BUTTER THIN BROWN BREAD. SPREAD WITH HONEY, THEN SPRINKLE WITH CHOPPED WALNUTS.

HONEY

CHRIS GARVEY.

NOW FOR SOME SAVOURY ONES, JUDY.

a CHOP HARD-BOILED EGGS AND GHERKINS. MIX TOGETHER WITH A LITTLE SALAD CREAM AND SPREAD ON WHITE, BUTTERED BREAD.

SALAD CREAM

b MASH SLICED LUNCHEON MEAT WITH CHOPPED PARSLEY AND PEELED TOMATO. SPREAD ON EITHER WHITE OR BROWN BREAD.

c Open Sandwiches
CUT A FRENCH LOAF DIAGONALLY TO MAKE LONG SLICES. CUT WELL-GRILLED SAUSAGES IN HALF LENGTHWAYS AND PUT ONE ON EACH SLICE. GARNISH WITH CHOPPED PICKLED-ONION AND LETTUCE.

NOW ARRANGE THE SANDWICHES ON SEP-ARATE DISHES, JUDY.

WHICH WILL YOU HAVE, FOLKS — SWEET OR SAVOURY?

MOTHER TELLS YOU HOW

TO MAKE **GINGER BEER**

MOTHER, GINGER BEER IS ONE OF MY FRIENDS' FAVOURITE DRINKS. CAN WE MAKE IT AT HOME?

YES, JUDY, OF COURSE WE CAN. IN FACT, IT'S VERY SIMPLE.

RECIPE
1½ LBS SUGAR
2 LEMONS
¼ OZ CREAM OF TARTAR
1 OZ ROOT GINGER — WELL BRUISED
1 HEAPED TABLE-SPOON OF BREWERS' YEAST
5 QUARTS OF BOILING WATER

FIRST OF ALL PEEL THE LEMONS VERY THINLY AND THEN REMOVE ALL THE PITH.

REMOVE ALL THE PITH.

CUT THE PEELED LEMONS INTO THIN SLICES AND PUT INTO A BOWL WITH THE PEEL AND ALL THE OTHER INGREDIENTS, EXCEPT THE YEAST.

NOW WE'LL ADD THE WATER AND LEAVE THE MIXTURE UNTIL IT IS JUST WARM.

5 QUARTS OF BOILING WATER.

THE LIQUID SHOULD BE LUKE-WARM, THAT IS ABOUT 98° FAHRENHEIT.

MIX IN THE YEAST AND LEAVE IN A WARM PLACE FOR 24 HOURS.

ADD YEAST

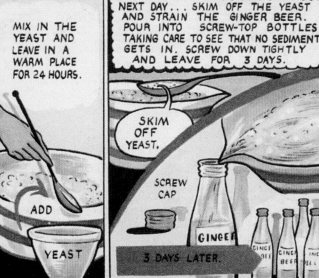

NEXT DAY... SKIM OFF THE YEAST AND STRAIN THE GINGER BEER. POUR INTO SCREW-TOP BOTTLES TAKING CARE TO SEE THAT NO SEDIMENT GETS IN. SCREW DOWN TIGHTLY AND LEAVE FOR 3 DAYS.

SKIM OFF YEAST.

SCREW CAP

GINGER

3 DAYS LATER.

COME AND HAVE SOME OF MY HOME-BREWED GINGER BEER!

5

MOTHER ON
HIGH DAYS, HOLIDAYS AND ENTERTAINING

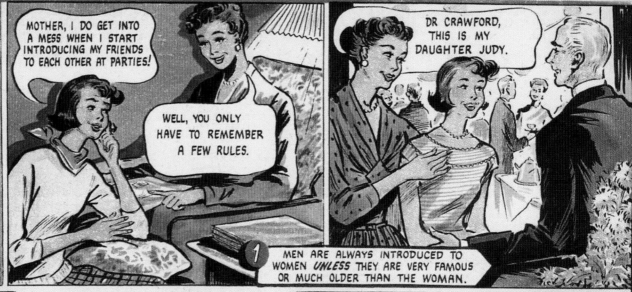

MOTHER TELLS YOU HOW

TO ARRANGE YOUR BIRTHDAY PARTY

WE'LL TAKE AWAY AS MUCH FURNITURE AS POSSIBLE, JUDY, SO THAT THERE'S PLENTY OF ROOM ROUND THE TABLE.

PLAN A COLD 'SUPPER' AND A BIG CAKE. CHOOSE A YELLOW, WHITE AND GREEN COLOUR SCHEME AND, FOR FUN, HAVE THE FOOD TO MATCH— SERVED ON TO PLATES AND READY TO EAT.

NOW FOR THE DECORATIONS, JUDY. FLOWERS ARE SCARCE SO WE'LL HAVE LITTLE BOWLS OF MIMOSA AND YELLOW AND WHITE JONQUILS.

FILL WHITE CEREAL BOWLS WITH WET SAND AND STICK IN THE FLOWERS WITH MIMOSA ALL ROUND THE EDGE. SAND KEEPS THEM FRESH AND ALSO HOLDS THEM IN POSITION.

Menu

Cold chicken with mixed veg. salad

*

Creamed sweet corn

*

Green salad

*

Baked jacket potatoes

*

Lemon mousse

*

Peach, apricot and pear jelly

*

Birthday cake

SET THE TABLE WITH A YELLOW CLOTH, GREEN PAPER NAPKINS AND WHITE CHINA. PLACE THE BOWLS OF FLOWERS ALONG THE CENTRE AND HAVE THE SWEET READY TO SERVE ON A SIDE TABLE.

HAPPY BIRTHDAY, JUDY. IF YOU BLOW OUT ALL THE CANDLES WITH ONE BREATH YOU CAN MAKE A WISH!

SERVE THE CAKE WITH TEA OR COFFEE AFTERWARDS. THE CAKE SHOULD BE MADE IN A BIG FLAN TIN SO THAT THERE'S PLENTY OF SPACE ON TOP FOR THE CANDLES.

IT WAS A LOVELY PARTY, BOTH OF YOU. YOU ARRANGED IT BEAUTIFULLY.

MOTHER TELLS YOU HOW

TO ENJOY BONFIRE NIGHT

JOHN AND MARY WANT TO BRING THEIR FIREWORKS HERE AS WE HAVE ROOM FOR A BONFIRE. MAY THEY, MOTHER?

OF COURSE, JUDY—AND WHY NOT ASK A FEW MORE FRIENDS, AS WELL, TO MAKE UP A SMALL PARTY?

ASK YOUR FRIENDS TO GATHER UP ALL THE OLD WOOD THEY CAN FIND FOR THE BONFIRE. IT MUST BE DRY.

TELL EVERYONE TO COME IN OLD COATS OR MACS AND WEAR GLOVES TO PROTECT THEIR HANDS FROM SPARKS.

CHOOSE A SAFE, OPEN SPOT FOR BUILDING THE BONFIRE. MAKE A FIRM FRAMEWORK OF THICK WOOD AND FILL IN WITH SMALLER PIECES AND WOOD-WOOL OR STRAW PACKING. SOAK A BOX OF SHAVINGS IN PARAFFIN AND PUT IT IN THE CENTRE JUST BEFORE LIGHTING THE FIRE. PILE THE REST OF THE WOOD ALL ROUND.

PUT TIM IN THE DINING-ROOM AWAY FROM THE NOISE. WE DON'T WANT TO FRIGHTEN HIM.

THE R.S.P.C.A. SAY ONE ASPIRIN FOR SMALL DOGS AND TWO FOR BIGGER ONES, LIKE LARGE TERRIERS, WILL SOOTHE THEM—ESPECIALLY IF THEY ARE KEPT OUT OF THE WAY AND OCCASIONALLY REASSURED.

PROTECTED NIGHTLIGHTS ARE THE BEST THINGS FOR LIGHTING HAND FIREWORKS. PUT SEVERAL IN SHALLOW TINS OUT OF THE WIND WHERE THEY ARE HANDY.

SERVE HOT SOUP AND SUBSTANTIAL SANDWICHES. LET EVERYONE STAND AROUND AND HELP THEMSELVES. THERE IS NO NEED TO PLAN AN ELABORATE MEAL AND HAVING IT IN THE KITCHEN SAVES EMBARRASSMENT OVER MUDDY SHOES AND OLD CLOTHES.

COME INTO THE KITCHEN, EVERYONE.

GOOD NIGHT, JUDY. THANK YOU FOR HAVING US—IT WAS LOVELY!

MOTHER TELLS YOU HOW

TO PLAN A HALLOWE'EN PARTY

JUDY, DON'T YOU THINK IT WOULD BE FUN TO HAVE A HALLOWE'EN PARTY THIS YEAR?

HALLOWE'EN IS THE EVE OF ALL HALLOWS, OR ALL SAINTS' DAY, WHICH IS THE FIRST OF NOVEMBER.

WE'LL MAKE OUR OWN INVITATION CARDS BY CUTTING THEM OUT OF STIFF PAPER AND PAINTING THEM TO LOOK LIKE ORANGE PUMPKINS.

PARTY

Come in Masks and Hats
To _____

ASK EVERYONE TO COME WEARING MASKS AND HATS.

DECORATE THE HOUSE WITH BAT AND GHOST SHAPES CUT OUT IN PAPER AND PAINTED WITH LUMINOUS PAINT.

THE MENU MUST BE IN KEEPING. WE'LL HAVE:

WITCHES' BREW
Mixed fruit juices with dabs of whipped white of egg on top.

GOBLIN PIE
Large covered dish containing roast potatoes and sausages.

FAIRY FINGERS
Light sponge, coloured green, topped with white icing and silver balls.

ROAST CHESTNUTS

TO RECEIVE THE GUESTS, JUDY, WE'LL DRESS YOU AS A WITCH IN A TALL HAT AND DARK CLOAK.

DON'T FORGET TO PLAY THE TRADITIONAL GAME OF 'BOB APPLE'. FILL A BATH WITH WATER AND FLOAT IN IT AN APPLE FOR EACH GUEST TO CAPTURE WITH HIS TEETH. IT'S GREAT FUN AS HANDS ARE NOT ALLOWED.

MOTHER TELLS YOU HOW

TO SEE THE NEW YEAR IN

1953
1954

WE'LL ASK THE AUNTS AND THE GRANDPARENTS TO SEE THE NEW YEAR IN WITH US, JUDY. WOULD YOU LIKE ONE OR TWO OF YOUR FRIENDS TO COME AS WELL?

YES PLEASE, MOTHER—BOB AND JILL, AT ANY RATE.

DISTRIBUTE "GOOD-LUCK" FAVOURS TO THE GUESTS AS THEY ARRIVE. CUT THEM OUT IN CARDBOARD AND COVER WITH COLOURED PAPER.

HAVE EASY-TO-EAT FOOD READY TO HAND ROUND AND FRUIT DRINKS POURED FOR 12 O'CLOCK.

PUT A BALLOON FOR EACH GUEST IN A NET SUSPENDED FROM THE CEILING, THEN AT 12 O'CLOCK UNDO THE STRING THAT KEEPS THEM IN THE NET, SO THAT THEY SHOWER DOWN ON THE PARTY.

HAPPY NEW YEAR EVERYONE!

ARRANGE FOR A DARK MAN TO BE THE "FIRST FOOTER" AND BRING IN WITH HIM A LUMP OF COAL TO PUT ON THE FIRE. THIS IS AN OLD CUSTOM WHICH IS MEANT TO BRING GOOD LUCK TO THE HOUSEHOLD FOR THE WHOLE OF THE NEXT YEAR.

SHOULD AULD ACQUAINTANCE BE FORGOT AND NEVER BROUGHT TO MIND... WE'LL TAKE A CUP OF KINDNESS YET, FOR THE SAKE OF AULD LANG SYNE.

THIS IS THE SONG TO REMIND YOU OF ABSENT FRIENDS AND MUST BE SUNG IN A COMPLETE CIRCLE WITH CROSSED ARMS.

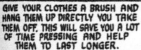

MOTHER TELLS YOU HOW

TO GIVE A BARBECUE

MOTHER, I WANT TO GIVE A PICNIC PARTY. CAN YOU THINK OF SOMETHING ORIGINAL?

YOU COULD ASK ONE OF THE BOYS TO HELP YOU, AND GIVE A BARBECUE PARTY, JUDY.

SUITABLE MENU

SAUSAGES
BACON
SALAD
ROLLS, CAKES
AND
SOFT DRINKS

NEVER BE TOO ELABORATE. 'SIMPLE, AND PLENTY OF IT' IS THE MOTTO.

BUILD A BRICK FIREPLACE LIKE THIS.

FIREPLACE MUST BE TWO BRICKS HIGH.

NOW YOU'LL NEED A GRILL, JUDY. I'LL LEND YOU A SHELF FROM THE OVEN.

REST GRILL FIRMLY ON THE BRICKS.

USE DRY WOOD FOR THE FIRE. MAKE SURE IT IS NOT SMOKING BEFORE YOU START COOKING

SERVE THE SAUSAGES AND BACON ON WOODEN SKEWERS. SALAD SHOULD BE CUT UP SO THAT PEOPLE CAN EAT IT WITH THEIR FINGERS.

MUSTARD

GOODBYE, JUDY, IT'S BEEN THE NICEST PARTY OF THE YEAR.

MOTHER TELLS YOU HOW

To make a T/v Snack

MOTHER, JILL AND BOB ARE GOING TO LOOK IN TOMORROW. WHAT CAN WE EAT?

WE'LL MAKE A DISH YOU CAN EAT WITH A FORK, JUDY.

GRATE HALF A POUND OF CHEDDAR CHEESE AND ONE LARGE ONION. FRY THE ONION WITH SEVERAL SLICED TOMATOES. ADD THE CHEESE AND MIX WELL.

NOW MIX IN THREE WELL-BEATEN EGGS AND COOK UNTIL THICK.

CUT SIX RASHERS OF STREAKY BACON INTO SMALL STRIPS AND FRY THEM CRISP, JUDY.

POUR THE CHEESE MIXTURE INTO CEREAL BOWLS, AND SPRINKLE WITH BACON

SERVE WITH FINGERS OF HOT, BUTTERED TOAST.

OH, JUDY, THIS IS LOVELY!

MOTHER TELLS YOU HOW

TO PACK A PICNIC LUNCH

DOROTHY HAS ASKED ME TO JOIN HER PICNIC PARTY. WE'RE ALL TAKING LUNCH WITH US.

HOW LOVELY, JUDY! WE'LL PLAN A MEAL FOR TWO PEOPLE SO THAT YOU CAN SHARE IF YOU WANT TO.

Menu

CHIPPOLATA SAUSAGES

CHEESE AND HAM SANDWICHES

LETTUCE HEARTS AND WATERCRESS

FRUIT IN JELLY

CAKE

LEMONADE OR COFFEE

STICK ALL THE SAUSAGES WITH COCKTAIL STICKS AND BE GENEROUS WITH THE SANDWICH FILLINGS, JUDY.

WASH THE LETTUCE HEARTS AND WATERCRESS, THEN DRY THEM IN A CLOTH. PACK IN A CLOSELY FITTING TIN. WRAP THE SAUSAGES AND SANDWICHES IN GREASEPROOF PAPER. CUT CAKE IN SLICES AND WRAP IN PAPER. PUT PIECES OF FRUIT IN ICE-CREAM CARTONS AND COVER WITH STIFFISH JELLY.

A STRAW BASKET IS THE BEST CARRIER. ONE END TAKES TWO THERMOS FLASKS (COMPLETE WITH CUPS) FOR COLD OR HOT DRINKS, ACCORDING TO TASTE. A SQUARE TIN FOR THE SANDWICHES, SAUSAGES AND CAKE GOES NEXT. PUT THE SMALL TIN OF SALAD AT THE BOTTOM OF THE REMAINING SPACE AND THE JELLIES ON TOP. STUFF ROUND WITH PAPER NAPKINS AND COVER WITH A PAPER TABLECLOTH. DON'T FORGET THE SPOONS FOR THE JELLIES.

PIN THE TABLECLOTH TO THE GRASS WITH FOUR SKEWERS OR TWIGS. LAY OUT THE FOOD ON THE NAPKINS AND GATHER UP EVERY SCRAP OF PAPER WHEN YOU FINISH.

GOOD-BYE, JOHN. IT WAS A LOVELY PICNIC AND THANK YOU FOR BRINGING ME HOME.

MOTHER TELLS YOU HOW

TO ENJOY A COUNTRY WALK

TAKE YOUR LIGHT-WEIGHT MAC, JUDY. IT WILL GO IN YOUR RUCKSACK.

WEAR STRONG SHOES AND LIGHT, ABSORBENT CLOTHES. TAKE A WOOLLIE TOO IN CASE THE WEATHER GETS COLD.

KEEP THE DISTANCE YOU PLAN TO WALK ON THE SHORT SIDE, THEN IF IT TURNS VERY HOT OR RAINS HARD YOU WON'T HAVE TO WORRY MUCH ABOUT GETTING BACK HOME.

PHEW, IT'S HOT! LET'S REST FOR A COUPLE OF HOURS UNDER THIS TREE.

AVOID WALKING IN THE HEAT. YOU WILL BE ABLE TO MAKE UP THE DELAY WHEN IT GETS COOLER AGAIN

IF A STORM COMES UP SHELTER IN A BARN OR UNDER A HEDGE IF YOU CAN. NEVER STAND UNDER TREES AS THEY ARE LIABLE TO BE STRUCK BY LIGHTNING.

SHUT THE GATE PROPERLY, BOB!

GATES LEFT OPEN CAN CAUSE FARMERS A LOT OF TROUBLE THROUGH CATTLE STRAYING. ANOTHER THING—SEE THAT ANY FIRES YOU MAKE ARE PUT OUT THOROUGHLY BEFORE YOU LEAVE.

SINGLE FILE HERE. WE MUSTN'T TRAMPLE THE CORN DOWN.

DID YOU ALL HAVE A GOOD TIME?

A WONDERFUL TIME, THANK YOU.

LOVELY, MOTHER. GOODNIGHT, EVERYONE!

MOTHER TELLS YOU HOW

TO PACK FOR A WEEKEND HOLIDAY

"MAKE A LIST OF THE THINGS YOU'LL NEED, JUDY, AND WE'LL TICK THEM OFF AS WE PACK."

PUT A LITTLE THOUGHT INTO YOUR PACKING — THERE IS NOTHING WORSE THAN HAVING TO BORROW BECAUSE YOU HAVE FORGOTTEN SOMETHING IMPORTANT.

THINGS TO TAKE WITH YOU

WARM COAT
THICK SHOES
MACKINTOSH
DRESS FOR EVENINGS
SHOES TO CHANGE
HANDKERCHIEFS
STOCKINGS
NIGHTWEAR
COMB AND BRUSH
SPONGE BAG

"A SMALL BAG AND A LIGHT CASE ARE BETTER THAN ONE REALLY HEAVY PIECE OF LUGGAGE, JUDY."

PACK NIGHT THINGS AND TOILET ARTICLES IN YOUR SMALL BAG AND THE REST OF YOUR THINGS IN THE SUITCASE.

IT'S BEST TO TRAVEL IN A WARM OUTFIT WHICH WILL DO FOR WALKS OUT OF DOORS. IT IS THE BULKIEST ITEM AND WEARING IT WILL LEAVE EXTRA ROOM IN YOUR CASE FOR OTHER THINGS.

"PUT YOUR SHOES IN CELLOPHANE BAGS AND DON'T FORGET THE BOX OF CHOCOLATES FOR YOUR HOSTESS."

THE BEST WAY TO PACK A SILK DRESS IS TO *ROLL* IT IN TISSUE PAPER. YOU WILL FIND THAT IT WILL SHAKE OUT QUITE UNCREASED.

"I'VE WRITTEN THE LABELS, MOTHER."

WRITE YOUR DESTINATION AND YOUR HOME ADDRESS ON THE LABELS AND TIE ON TO EACH PIECE OF LUGGAGE.

"GOOD-BYE!"

"HAVE A GOOD TIME, JUDY. WE'LL MEET YOUR TRAIN WHEN YOU RETURN."

MOTHER TELLS YOU HOW

HOW TO CAMP IN COMFORT

MOTHER, HAVE YOU ANY IDEAS FOR OUR CLUB CAMPING WEEK?

YES, JUDY—THE MOST IMPORTANT THING IS TO MAKE YOURSELF AS COMFORTABLE AS POSSIBLE.

FIRST OF ALL, YOUR BED: A WATERPROOF GROUND-SHEET, A COTTON SLEEPING-BAG AND FOUR BLANKETS ARE ESSENTIAL.

GROUND-SHEET

1

BLANKET Nº 1

SLEEPING BAG

BLANKET Nº 2

2

BLANKET Nº 3

BLANKETS 1 & 2 FOLDED OVER SLEEPING BAG

BLANKET Nº 4

3

THICKNESS *UNDERNEATH* IS THE SECRET OF COMFORT. LAY YOUR BED OUT LIKE THIS.

KITCHEN SHELTER

CHOOSE A WELL-DRAINED PITCH FOR YOUR TENT, WITH SHELTER FROM THE PREVAILING WIND. USE THE TENT TO SHELTER THE KITCHEN, UNLESS YOU ARE COOKING WITH AN OPEN FIRE.

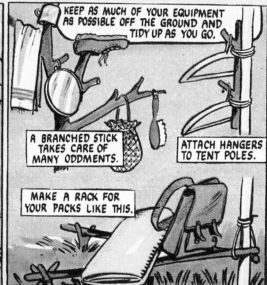

KEEP AS MUCH OF YOUR EQUIPMENT AS POSSIBLE OFF THE GROUND AND TIDY UP AS YOU GO.

A BRANCHED STICK TAKES CARE OF MANY ODDMENTS.

ATTACH HANGERS TO TENT POLES.

MAKE A RACK FOR YOUR PACKS LIKE THIS.

HAVE A GOOD TIME, GIRLS, AND REMEMBER— NO LITTER!

MOTHER TELLS YOU HOW

TO MAKE A VALENTINE

MOTHER, DO YOU KNOW WHERE TO GET A VALENTINE CARD? BILL WANTS ONE.

IF YOU LIKE, I'LL SHOW YOU HOW TO *MAKE* ONE.

WE'LL NEED SOME BRIGHT PINK PAPER AND A LACEY PAPER DOYLEY.

ST VALENTINE'S DAY — THE 14th FEBRUARY — IS THE TRADITIONAL DAY FOR SENDING A CARD TO ANYONE YOU ADMIRE. IT MUST BE ANONYMOUS AND SHOULD HAVE A LITTLE VERSE INSIDE.

CUT OUT DOUBLE PAPER IN THE SHAPE OF A JOINED HEART AS SHOWN. MAKE A PAPER PATTERN FIRST TO GET IT RIGHT.

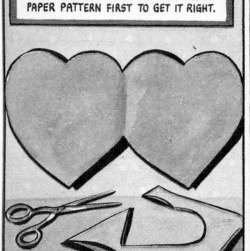

OUTLINE THE EDGE OF THE CARD WITH A FRILL OF PAPER LACE TAKEN FROM THE DOYLEY.

GLUE FRILL NEATLY TO BACK OF THE CARD, AS SHOWN.

BACK

WRITE IN GOLD ON THE FRONT — *TO MY VALENTINE* — AND INSIDE A VERSE SUCH AS THE ONE BELOW:-

TO MY VALENTINE

ROSES ARE RED AND VIOLETS BLUE, SUGAR IS SWEET AND SO ARE YOU.

OH, JUDY, I WONDER WHO SENT THIS TO ME?

MOTHER TELLS YOU HOW

TO MAKE EASTER NOVELTIES

WE'LL MAKE SOME EASTER CARDS THIS YEAR, JUDY, TO GIVE TO OUR FRIENDS.

APRIL 16

YES, AND COULDN'T WE DO SOMETHING SPECIAL FOR BREAKFAST ON EASTER SUNDAY?

A QUICK AND EFFECTIVE CARD CAN BE MADE BY FOLDING A PIECE OF PAPER IN HALF, THEN STICKING A SPRING FLOWER PRINT IN THE CENTRE OF THE FRONT PAGE. FOR AN AMUSING EGG-AND-CHICKEN CARD, MAKE A DOUBLE OVAL IN GREEN CARDBOARD, THEN CUT OUT THE EDGES AS SHOWN. STICK A YELLOW CHICKEN SHAPE ON THE UNDER OVAL AND PAINT IN LEGS, WINGS, BEAK AND EYES.

HAPPY EASTER

Easter Greetings

FOR EASTER SUNDAY BREAKFAST, COLOUR WHITE EGGS WITH CULINARY DYES — COCHINEAL, SAP GREEN AND SAFFRON YELLOW — BY PUTTING A LITTLE OF THE DYE IN THE WATER WHEN YOU BOIL THE EGGS.

I'LL MAKE EASTER BONNETS FOR THE EGGS, MOTHER.

4½" 1¼ 1½" 1½" ½" ½" 1½"

CUT OUT CREPE PAPER (AS DIAGRAM) AND STICK THE EDGES TOGETHER AND THE FRILL IN PLACE WITH ADHESIVE TAPE. HAVE THE BONNETS READY AND, WHEN THE EGGS ARE COOKED, DRAW IN THE FACES WITH INK, THEN STICK THE BONNETS IN PLACE WITH TINY TABS OF THE ADHESIVE TAPE.

YOUNGSTERS WILL LOVE LITTLE BASKETS OF MARZIPAN EGGS.

RECIPE

¼ lb of ground almonds.

¼ lb of icing sugar.

The white of 1 egg.

A little sap green colouring.

BEAT THE WHITE THOROUGHLY AND ADD THE GROUND ALMONDS, SUGAR AND COLOURING. MIX WELL, THEN SHAPE INTO "EGGS". ROLL EACH IN A VERY LITTLE CASTOR SUGAR.

CUT IN HALF, THESE EGGS CAN ALSO BE USED TO DECORATE AN EASTER CAKE.

MOTHER TELLS YOU HOW

TO MAKE LAST-MINUTE CHRISTMAS GIFTS

"AUNTIE MARY HAS BEEN SO GOOD TO ME, MOTHER, THAT I WOULD LIKE TO GIVE HER AN EXTRA SPECIAL PRESENT."

"SHE LOVES LITTLE HATS, JUDY, SO WHY NOT TRIM A FUR FELT FOR HER? YOU CAN BUY A PLAIN SHAPE FOR ABOUT TEN SHILLINGS."

SEW PEARL BEADS ROUND THE CROWN AND WORK A LITTLE DESIGN OF THEM IN THE FRONT.

"ALL YOUR CLUB AND SCHOOL FRIENDS COULD HAVE BOOK-MARKERS MADE FROM CORDED RIBBON."

CHOOSE THICK CORDED RIBBON ABOUT HALF AN INCH WIDE AND FRINGE OUT THE ENDS. IF YOU HAVE TIME, EMBROIDER A LITTLE SPRAY OF FLOWERS AT EACH END.

"BOB COLLECTS CHEESE LABELS, DOESN'T HE? WHY NOT MAKE HIM A BOOK TO STICK THEM IN BY COVERING AN EXERCISE OR ACCOUNTS BOOK WITH GAY PATTERNED PAPER?"

TO COVER, CUT PAPER LIKE THIS, ALLOWING 2 TO 3 INCHES ALL ROUND.

TURN THE PAPER TO THE INSIDE AND STICK DOWN FIRMLY. COVER THE CENTRE WITH PLAIN PAPER, IF NEEDED, AND STICK A LABEL ON THE FRONT COVER.

MAKE SOME BRIGHT LITTLE HANGING TOYS FOR THE BABIES.

CUT OUT SHAPES IN STIFF CARDBOARD AND COVER THEM WITH METALLIC PAPER. TRIM WITH STUCK-ON SEQUINS. SUSPEND ALL THE PIECES ON NYLON THREAD SO THAT WHEN THE TOYS ARE HUNG UP THEY MOVE ABOUT AND GLITTER.

"I'LL HELP YOU DO UP THE PRESENTS, JUDY — THE PACKING IS ALMOST AS IMPORTANT AS THE GIFT."

CHOOSE BRIGHT, SHINING MATERIALS FOR CHRISTMAS PACKING AND DO UP THE PARCELS WITH TINSEL-TAPE OR RIBBON.

MOTHER TELLS YOU HOW

TO DECORATE FOR THE CORONATION

YOU HELP DADDY MAKE A SKETCH OF THE HOUSE, JUDY, THEN WE CAN SEE HOW IT LOOKS.

THERE'S NO NEED TO KEEP TO A RED, WHITE AND BLUE COLOUR SCHEME. ANY BRIGHT COLOURS WILL GIVE THE HOUSE A GAY, FESTIVE AIR.

HERE'S THE SKETCH JUDY'S FATHER MADE. HE WILL PLANT THE WINDOW BOXES WITH CALCEOLARIAS, LOBELIA AND GERANIUMS. JUDY WILL MAKE A LAUREL GARLAND FOR THE DOOR, TIPPING THE LEAVES WITH GOLD PAINT AND THEN WIRING THE GOLD CROWN AND E.R. INTO POSITION.

COME AND SEE THE DOORWAY, MOTHER!

PAPER OR BUNTING 'DRAPES' ROUND THE DOOR FRAMES LOOK VERY GAY AND WELCOMING. THEY CAN BE BOUGHT CHEAPLY IN MOST BIG CHAIN STORES.

BABY WILL LOVE *THIS* DECORATION, JUDY.

STICK A CUT-OUT STATE COACH AND HORSES ALONG THE BOTTOM OF THE OVERMANTEL MIRROR AND OUTLINE THE FRAME WITH A STRIP OF CRINKLED PAPER.

AND WHY NOT HAVE A CORONATION TEA PARTY WITH A HUGE CORONATION CAKE?

MOTHER TELLS YOU HOW

TO DECORATE FOR CHRISTMAS

I'VE BOUGHT VARIEGATED HOLLY, JUDY—IT LOOKS MUCH MORE FESTIVE THAN THE DARK GREEN KIND. WE'LL MASS IT ABOVE THE PICTURES AND OVER THE MIRROR.

NEVER AGAIN WILL I HAVE OUR CHRISTMAS CARDS STANDING ON THE MANTELPIECE. THEY ALWAYS FALL DOWN.

STICK OR PIN THE CARDS TO STRIPS OF BRIGHT RED OR GREEN PAPER AND HANG THEM EACH SIDE OF THE FIREPLACE.

ANOTHER GOOD WAY OF DEALING WITH CARDS IS TO HANG THEM OVER TINSEL RIBBON STRETCHED ALONG THE WALL.

THAT WICKER FLOWER BASKET LOOKS LOVELY FILLED WITH HOLLY AND MISTLETOE.

"SNOWFLAKE" GARLANDS (LIKE THE ONE JUDY IS HOLDING) ARE QUICK TO MAKE BY THREADING TUFTS OF COTTON WOOL ON TO NYLON THREAD. THEY CAN THEN BE HUNG OVER THE WINDOWS.

DECORATE THE TABLE WITH LONG STRIPS OF CHRISTMAS PAPER. FOR THE CENTRE PANEL, STICK STUBBY RED CANDLES ON TO SMALL SILVER CAKE BOARDS AND ARRANGE SPRIGS OF HOLLY ALL ROUND.

MAKE A HOLLY WREATH TIED WITH RED RIBBON FOR THE FRONT DOOR. IT LOOKS GAY AND WELCOMING WHEN YOUR FRIENDS CALL TO SAY "MERRY CHRISTMAS!"

MOTHER TELLS YOU HOW

TO MAKE TWO PARTY DRINKS

MOTHER, WHAT NEW DRINKS CAN I HAVE FOR MY PARTY THIS YEAR?

I THINK YOU SHOULD HAVE ONE COLD AND ONE HOT ONE, JUDY.

BLACKCURRANT MILK (COLD)

YOU WILL NEED:— 1 QUART OF MILK, 4 TABLESPOONS OF BLACKCURRANT JUICE.

STIR THE JUICE INTO THE MILK A LITTLE AT A TIME. ADD ICE.

WE'LL SERVE THIS FROM BIG GLASS JUGS — IT LOOKS MOST EXCITING.

NOW FOR OUR HOT DRINK — WE'LL HAVE A SPICY FRUIT PUNCH.

SPICED PUNCH (HOT)

YOU WILL NEED:—

QUARTER PINT OF GINGER CORDIAL. 1 PT. ORANGE SQUASH. ½ TEASPOON CINNAMON. HOT WATER.

GINGER CORDIAL

ORANGE SQUASH

CINNAMON

MAKE UP THE ORANGE SQUASH AS EXPLAINED ON THE BOTTLE, USING HOT WATER. ADD THE GINGER CORDIAL AND THE CINNAMON. REHEAT AND PUT INTO A PUNCH BOWL. SERVE IN CUPS USING A LADLE.

DO HAVE A HOT NIGHTCAP BEFORE YOU GO, EVERYBODY!

6

MOTHER TELLS YOU HOW

TO MAKE A CUSHION COVER

I'D LOVE TO MAKE TWO BRIGHT CUSHION COVERS FOR MY ROOM, MOTHER.

I KNOW! THAT PIECE OF FLOWERED COTTON LEFT OVER FROM YOUR SKIRT IS JUST THE THING!

HALF A YARD OF 36" MATERIAL CUT IN TWO WILL MAKE THE FRONTS OF TWO CUSHION COVERS.

FIRST, COUCH ALL ROUND THE CENTRE AND CORNER FLOWERS WITH CANDLEWICK COTTON, JUDY.

COUCHING

WE'LL BACK THE MATERIAL WITH PLAIN YELLOW COTTON TO MATCH THE EMBROIDERY.

ZIP

ON THEIR WRONG SIDES, SEW FRONT (PATTERNED) AND BACK (PLAIN) PIECES TOGETHER, LEAVING ONE SIDE FREE. TURN AND SEW A ZIP FASTENER INTO THE OPENING.

NOW FOR THE PROFESSIONAL FINISH—A TUFTED FRINGE ALL ROUND THE EDGE.

TUFTING

A B C

THE FRINGE IS MADE FROM 3" LENGTHS OF CANDLEWICK COTTON. WORK THE TUFTS VERY CLOSE ALL ROUND. FIT THE COVER OVER A CUSHION.

WHAT FUN, JUDY— THE CUSHIONS MATCH YOUR SKIRT!

MOTHER TELLS YOU HOW

TO MAKE A

Waste-Paper-Basket

MOTHER, I WOULD LIKE A PRETTY WASTE-PAPER-BASKET FOR MY ROOM.

WE'LL MAKE ONE TO MATCH YOUR WALL, JUDY.

ASK YOUR LOCAL SWEET SHOP TO SELL YOU A TIN — IT CAN BE CYLINDRICAL OR SQUARE, BUT SHOULD BE FAIRLY LARGE.

FELT

YOU WILL ALSO NEED A PIECE OF FELT AND SOME BOBBLE FRINGE.

NOW WE'LL WANT THAT ROLL OF PAPER LEFT OVER FROM DOING UP YOUR ROOM, JUDY.

CUT THE PAPER TO FIT THE TIN AND STICK IT ON, NEATLY TURNING IT OVER AT THE EDGE.

COVER THE INSIDE EDGE WITH PAPER TAPE OR BRAID.

CUT THE FELT TO FIT THE BOTTOM, JUDY, THEN STICK IT ON.

FELT BASE.

NOW FOR THE TRIMMING — STICK THE BOBBLE FRINGE ALL ROUND THE TOP OF THE TIN.

WHY, IT MATCHES YOUR ROOM PERFECTLY, JUDY!

MOTHER TELLS YOU HOW

TO MODERNISE AN OLD CHEST OF DRAWERS

MOTHER, WHAT CAN I DO WITH THAT OLD CHEST IN MY ROOM?

WE CAN CHEER IT UP A LOT, JUDY!

FIRST OF ALL WE'LL GIVE IT TWO COATS OF WHITE ENAMEL.

NOW WE'LL GET A MIRROR. MIRROR-GLASS IS NOT EXPENSIVE AND CAN BE BOUGHT IN ANY SIZE.

CONSULT YOUR HARDWARE MERCHANT ABOUT THIS AND ASK HIM TO DRILL HOLES FOR FIXING IT IN POSITION.

NOW, FOR THE FINISHING TOUCH, WE'LL USE STRIPS OF THIS IVY-PATTERNED WALL PAPER.

STICK A CUT-OUT BORDER ALL ROUND THE MIRROR AND SEPARATE LEAVES ON THE DRAWERS.

GLUE

PAINT OVER THE PAPER WITH PAPER VARNISH.

PAPER VARNISH

OH, JUDY, THAT DOES LOOK PRETTY AGAINST YOUR PLAIN WALLS!

MOTHER TELLS YOU HOW

TO MODERNIZE A CHAIR

MOTHER, I WOULD LIKE TO HAVE ANOTHER CHAIR IN MY ROOM. THERE'S NOWHERE FOR MY FRIENDS TO SIT WHEN THEY COME TO SEE ME.

THERE ARE SEVERAL OLD CHAIRS IN THE ATTIC, JUDY. WE'LL MODERNIZE ONE OF THOSE.

OH, I DON'T WANT ANYTHING LIKE THAT, MOTHER!

WAIT UNTIL YOU SEE WHAT CAN BE DONE TO IT, JUDY.

FIRST OF ALL, CUT THE LEGS DOWN TO FOURTEEN INCHES.

14"

CUT HERE.

THIS REMNANT OF SCARLET DOT MATERIAL WILL BE VERY GAY IN YOUR ROOM—2½ YARDS WILL BE PLENTY. NOW WE'LL START BY MAKING A PADDED BACK FOR THE CHAIR.

YOU WILL NEED — COVERING MATERIAL, THICK WADDING, STIFF MUSLIN, DRAWING PINS, ELASTIC, AND A CIRCULAR RUBBER CUSHION.

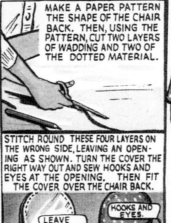

MAKE A PAPER PATTERN THE SHAPE OF THE CHAIR BACK. THEN, USING THE PATTERN, CUT TWO LAYERS OF WADDING AND TWO OF THE DOTTED MATERIAL.

STITCH ROUND THESE FOUR LAYERS ON THE WRONG SIDE, LEAVING AN OPENING AS SHOWN. TURN THE COVER THE RIGHT WAY OUT AND SEW HOOKS AND EYES AT THE OPENING. THEN FIT THE COVER OVER THE CHAIR BACK.

LEAVE OPEN

HOOKS AND EYES.

ELASTIC

OH, JUDY, WHAT A LOVELY NEW CHAIR!

MAKE A FRILL 13" × 72" AND LINE IT WITH STIFF MUSLIN. THREAD ELASTIC THROUGH THE TOP. PIN IN POSITION ROUND THE SEAT OF THE CHAIR WITH COLOURED DRAWING PINS. FASTEN THE ELASTIC AND SEAM THE FRILL UP THE BACK. COVER A CIRCULAR RUBBER CUSHION TO MATCH.

DRAWING PINS

MOTHER TELLS YOU HOW

TO MAKE A FIRESIDE "TUFFET"
*

JILL HAS SUCH A COMFORTABLE "TUFFET" IN HER ROOM, MOTHER.

I'LL SHOW YOU HOW TO MAKE ONE FOR YOURSELF IF YOU LIKE, JUDY.

YOU WILL NEED SEVEN DRIED MILK TINS, SOME OLD STOCKINGS OR SOCKS, WADDING, STRING, PLASTIC GLUE AND ABOUT 1 YD. OF COVERING MATERIAL.

NOW'S OUR CHANCE TO USE UP THE EMPTY DRIED MILK TINS AND YOUR OLD SCHOOL STOCKINGS!

FIRST, COVER EACH TIN WITH A LENGTH OF STOCKING, GATHERING THE ENDS UP TIGHTLY, TOP AND BOTTOM, AS SHOWN IN THE DIAGRAM.

NEXT SEW THE COVERED TINS TOGETHER WITH ONE TIN IN THE MIDDLE AND THE OTHER SIX ROUND IT.

USE A CURVED PACKING NEEDLE

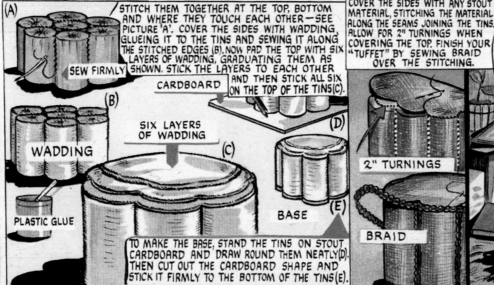

(A) SEW FIRMLY

STITCH THEM TOGETHER AT THE TOP, BOTTOM AND WHERE THEY TOUCH EACH OTHER — SEE PICTURE 'A'. COVER THE SIDES WITH WADDING, GLUEING IT TO THE TINS AND SEWING IT ALONG THE STITCHED EDGES (B). NOW PAD THE TOP WITH SIX LAYERS OF WADDING, GRADUATING THEM AS SHOWN. STICK THE LAYERS TO EACH OTHER AND THEN STICK ALL SIX ON THE TOP OF THE TINS (C).

CARDBOARD

(B) WADDING

PLASTIC GLUE

SIX LAYERS OF WADDING

(C)

(D)

BASE (E)

TO MAKE THE BASE, STAND THE TINS ON STOUT CARDBOARD AND DRAW ROUND THEM NEATLY (D). THEN CUT OUT THE CARDBOARD SHAPE AND STICK IT FIRMLY TO THE BOTTOM OF THE TINS (E).

COVER THE SIDES WITH ANY STOUT MATERIAL, STITCHING THE MATERIAL ALONG THE SEAMS JOINING THE TINS. ALLOW FOR 2" TURNINGS WHEN COVERING THE TOP. FINISH YOUR "TUFFET" BY SEWING BRAID OVER THE STITCHING.

2" TURNINGS

BRAID

DO COME IN, JILL, AND SIT BY THE FIRE!

110

MOTHER TELLS YOU HOW

TO MAKE A SHELF-TIDY

I DON'T KNOW WHAT TO DO WITH ALL THESE SMALL ODDS AND ENDS, MOTHER.

KEEPING SMALL THINGS IN ORDER IS A PROBLEM, JUDY. WHY NOT TURN YOUR BOTTOM BOOK-SHELF INTO A "TIDY"?

I'VE BEEN SAVING THESE HONEY JARS WITH THE SCREW TOP LIDS AND THEY'RE THE VERY THING FOR THE JOB.

CHOOSE WELL-SHAPED JARS WITH CLOSE-FITTING SCREW LIDS.

JUDY, YOU MARK OUT THE SHELF SO THAT THE JARS WILL BE EVENLY SPACED.

PUNCH TWO HOLES IN EACH LID WITH A NAIL.

LID SHOWING SCREWS

SCREW THE LIDS TO THE SHELF THROUGH THE HOLES ALREADY PIERCED.

THE JARS CAN BE PLACED QUITE CLOSE TOGETHER AND WILL TAKE UP VERY LITTLE ROOM.

THEY DO LOOK PRETTY NOW YOU'VE PAINTED THEM, JUDY, AND THEY'LL BE USEFUL TOO!

YES. I'M GOING TO MAKE ANOTHER SET FOR MOTHER TO USE IN THE KITCHEN.

MOTHER TELLS YOU HOW

TO MAKE A SHELF-CABINET

I WOULD LIKE A LITTLE CUPBOARD FOR MY ODDMENTS, MOTHER.

THERE IS PLENTY OF ROOM IN YOUR BOOKSHELVES FOR ONE.

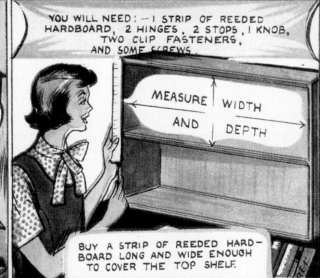

YOU WILL NEED: — 1 STRIP OF REEDED HARDBOARD, 2 HINGES, 2 STOPS, 1 KNOB, TWO CLIP FASTENERS, AND SOME SCREWS.

MEASURE WIDTH AND DEPTH

BUY A STRIP OF REEDED HARD-BOARD LONG AND WIDE ENOUGH TO COVER THE TOP SHELF.

NOW MARK OUT THE DOOR ON THE BACK OF THE HARDBOARD, JUDY.

FRET-SAW

CUT WITH A FRET-SAW — YOUR PIECES WILL LOOK LIKE THIS.

SCREW THE FRAME AT EACH CORNER TO THE SHELF.

OH, WHAT A GOOD IDEA, JUDY.

SCREW THE HINGES IN POSITION AND STICK STOPS UNDER THE TOP EDGE. FIX THE CLIP FASTENERS IN THE DOOR BELOW THE STOPS AND SCREW IN THE KNOB — PAINT TO MATCH THE SHELVES.

MOTHER TELLS YOU HOW

TO LAY A COLOURED FLOOR

114

MOTHER TELLS YOU HOW

TO PAINT YOUR ROOM

MOTHER, CAN WE DO MY ROOM UP? I WOULD LIKE A NEW COLOUR SCHEME — THE CEILING AND WALL BEHIND MY BED IN SOFT GREEN AND THE REST IN ROSE PINK.

YES, OF COURSE WE CAN. WE'LL STRIP THE WALLS AND CEILING AND PAINT THEM BOTH.

FIRST OF ALL CLEAR THE ROOM OF FURNITURE, CARPETS, CURTAINS ETC. TO REACH THE CEILING YOU WILL NEED A STOUT TABLE OR TWO PAIRS OF STEPS AND A BOARD.

COVER YOUR HAIR WITH A CLEAN DUSTER, JUDY—YOU DON'T WANT SPOTS OF PAINT ALL OVER IT. WE SHALL NEED PLENTY OF HOT WATER TO WET THE PAPER THOROUGHLY THEN WE CAN LEAVE IT FOR A LITTLE WHILE TO LOOSEN.

USE OLD DISTEMPER BRUSHES FOR WETTING THE PAPER—YOU WILL NEED STRIPPING KNIVES TO GET THE WALL PERFECTLY CLEAN.

CAREFUL JUDY— DON'T DIG THE KNIFE INTO THE WALL—RESOAK ANY STUBBORN PIECES.

GOOD — THE SURFACE IS PERFECT. IT'S LUCKY THERE ARE NO HOLES TO FILL UP BEFORE THE PAINTING.

ROLLERS ARE THE BEST THINGS FOR PAINTING LARGE SURFACES AND EMULSION PAINT IS EASY TO USE WITH THEM.

EMULSION PAINT

DO THE CEILING FIRST AND WORK IN ROUGH CRISS-CROSS STROKES OF THE ROLLER. COMPLETE THE WHOLE CEILING AT ONE GO OR YOU MAY HAVE A MARK WHERE THE PAINT HAS DRIED.

NOW FOR THE PINK WALLS — WE CAN TIDY UP EDGES AND THE DIFFICULT PARTS WITH A BRUSH AS WE GO.

JUDY, HOW LOVELY.

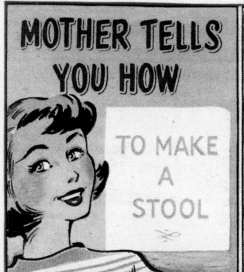

MOTHER TELLS YOU HOW

TO MAKE A STOOL

MOTHER, CAN YOU THINK OF A WAY TO MAKE A STOOL FOR MY ROOM?

YES, JUDY — ON THE SAME LINES AS YOUR 'LONG JOHN' TABLE.

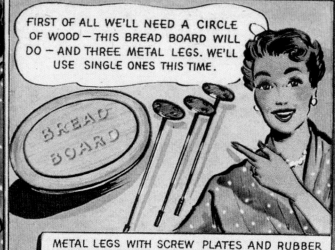

FIRST OF ALL WE'LL NEED A CIRCLE OF WOOD — THIS BREAD BOARD WILL DO — AND THREE METAL LEGS. WE'LL USE SINGLE ONES THIS TIME.

BREAD BOARD

METAL LEGS WITH SCREW PLATES AND RUBBER FEET CAN BE BOUGHT IN 9" AND 18" LENGTHS. YOU WILL NEED THREE.

MARK OUT THE POSITION FOR EACH, AND SCREW IN PLACE.

MARKING FOR SCREWS

NOW WE'LL COVER THE TOP WITH FOAM-RUBBER.

FOAM-RUBBER

RUBBER SOLUTION

BUY A CIRCLE OR A SQUARE AND CUT IT WITH SCISSORS TO FIT THE TOP. STICK TO THE WOOD WITH RUBBER SOLUTION.

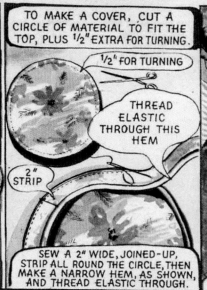

TO MAKE A COVER, CUT A CIRCLE OF MATERIAL TO FIT THE TOP, PLUS 1/2" EXTRA FOR TURNING.

1/2" FOR TURNING

THREAD ELASTIC THROUGH THIS HEM

2" STRIP

SEW A 2" WIDE, JOINED-UP, STRIP ALL ROUND THE CIRCLE, THEN MAKE A NARROW HEM, AS SHOWN, AND THREAD ELASTIC THROUGH.

THIS STOOL IS JOLLY HANDY FOR BOTH IN AND OUT OF DOORS.

MOTHER TELLS YOU HOW

to Re-seat a Chair

OH! I'VE GONE THROUGH THE SEAT OF THE CHAIR.

NEVER MIND, JUDY. WE'LL SOON REPAIR IT.

WE'LL USE RESILIENT WEBBING. IT IS SOLD BY THE YARD, AND WE'LL NEED FOUR AND A HALF YARDS.

TWO LARGE-HEADED TACKS ARE NEEDED FOR EACH END OF EACH STRIP.

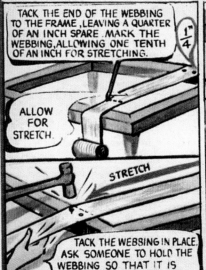

TACK THE END OF THE WEBBING TO THE FRAME, LEAVING A QUARTER OF AN INCH SPARE. MARK THE WEBBING, ALLOWING ONE TENTH OF AN INCH FOR STRETCHING.

1" / 4

ALLOW FOR STRETCH.

STRETCH

TACK THE WEBBING IN PLACE. ASK SOMEONE TO HOLD THE WEBBING SO THAT IT IS STRETCHED FOR YOU TO TACK.

CUT

PLAIT THE WEBBING AS YOU GO. IT SHOULD LOOK LIKE THIS WHEN FINISHED.

NOW WE'LL NEED A PLASTIC FOAM CUSHION, JUDY. LET'S COVER IT TO MATCH THE SOFA.

SLIP-OVER COVER

WHAT DO YOU THINK OF MY UPHOLSTERY, JILL?

MOTHER TELLS YOU HOW

TO MAKE A PELMET

MOTHER, DO YOU THINK I COULD HAVE A NEW PELMET FOR MY ROOM?

YES, OF COURSE, JUDY. WE'LL MAKE ONE OF HARDBOARD.

FIRST OF ALL, MEASURE THE WIDTH OF THE WINDOW ACROSS THE FRAME. THEN WE'LL GO AND BUY THE BOARD.

TOP

5"

YOU WILL NEED ¼" THICK HARDBOARD AS FOLLOWS:—
TWO STRIPS 5" DEEP AND THE WIDTH OF THE WINDOW FOR THE TOP AND FRONT OF THE PELMET.
TWO 5" SQUARES FOR THE SIDES.
TWO 5" LONG PIECES OF 1 INCH QUARTERING.
8 PANEL PINS.
2 PAIRS OF SCREW HOOKS.
EVO-STIK.

FIRST STICK THE QUARTERING TO THE END OF ONE OF THE LONG STRIPS. THEN STICK THE SIDE PIECES IN PLACE.

QUARTERING

STICK QUARTERING AT EACH END

'QUARTERING' IS SQUARED WOOD

EVO-STIK

5"

5"

FIX END PIECES

NOW WE'LL FIX ON THE OTHER LONG STRIP AS THE TOP, JUDY. STICK IT IN POSITION FIRST, THEN HAMMER IN THE PINS.

PANEL PINS.

HOOK

TO FIX TO THE WINDOW, SCREW A SMALL EYE INTO THE TOP OF THE WINDOW FRAME EACH SIDE, AND A MATCHING HOOK INTO THE PELMET.

I'LL COVER MY PELMET WITH WALL-PAPER TO MATCH THE WALL, MOTHER.

YOU *ARE* GOING 'CONTEMPORARY', JUDY.

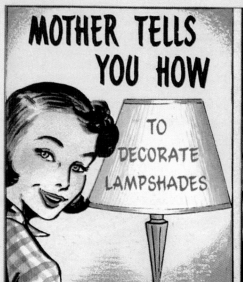

MOTHER TELLS YOU HOW

TO DECORATE LAMPSHADES

I'VE BOUGHT THESE PLAIN LAMPSHADES FOR YOUR ROOM, JUDY, SO THAT WE CAN DECORATE THEM TO MATCH YOUR COVERS.

WE'LL USE ODDMENTS OF FELT AND CUT OUT LITTLE FLOWERS IN YELLOW, SCARLET AND PALE BLUE.

PUT A DAB OF PLASTIC GLUE ON THE BACK OF EACH AND STICK IT INTO POSITION ON THE SHADE.

NOW ADD A MATCHING BORDER OF SMALL FELT TRIANGLES.

DECORATE THE HANGING LAMPSHADE TO MATCH, BUT MAKE THE FLOWERS A BIT LARGER.

OTHER PRETTY FELT DESIGNS:

CIRCLES WITH CUT-OUT SPOTS IN THE CENTRE LOOK ATTRACTIVE. SO DO FELT CHERRIES WITH A MATCHING BALL-FRINGE EDGING.

WE MUST START THINKING ABOUT CHRISTMAS PRESENTS VERY SOON, MOTHER.

YES! IT WOULD BE A GOOD IDEA TO DECORATE A TEA COSY IN THE SAME WAY AS THE LAMPSHADES FOR AUNT MARY.

7 MOTHER'S FINISHING TOUCHES

MOTHER TELLS YOU HOW

TO MAKE WINTER FLOWER DECORATIONS

FLOWERS ARE SO EXPENSIVE NOW, MOTHER, AND THEY ONLY LAST SUCH A SHORT TIME!

WELL, YOU CAN MAKE A VERY PRETTY DECORATION WITH OUR DRIED FLOWERS, JUDY, AND THEY'LL LAST FOR AGES.

THERE, JUDY— ALL OUR FLOWERS AND LEAVES ARE DRY NOW AND THEY LOOK LOVELY.

ALMOST ALL FLOWERS AND LEAVES CAN BE DRIED SUCCESSFULLY, BUT THE FOLLOWING GIVE THE BEST RESULTS: POPPY HEADS, STATICE, DELPHINIUMS, HYDRANGEAS AND YARROW. ALL YOU HAVE TO DO IS HANG THE FLOWERS UP AS YOU SEE IN THE PICTURE AND LEAVE THEM TO DRY FOR THREE WEEKS TO A MONTH.

NOW, FILL THE BOAT-SHAPED VASE WITH SAND, JUDY.

USE FAIRLY COARSE, DRY SAND TO SUPPORT THE FLOWERS.

ARRANGE THE SPRAYS SO THAT THE HEAVY ONES ARE AT THE BOTTOM.

WHAT A WONDERFUL DECORATION, JUDY!

ISN'T IT NICE? WE MADE IT FROM FLOWERS WE HAD DRIED OURSELVES.

123

MOTHER TELLS YOU HOW

TO PRESS FLOWERS

AREN'T THEY LOVELY, MOTHER? I FOUND THEM ON OUR WALK.

YES, JUDY! WHY DON'T YOU KEEP ONE OF EACH FOR A WILD FLOWER COLLECTION.

FLOWERS FOR JUNE AND JULY

BUTTERCUP
DAISY
SPEEDWELL
CAMPION
RAGGED ROBIN
MALLOW
MEADOW SWEET
HEARTSEASE
SHEPHERD'S PURSE
VETCH

YOU WILL NEED PLENTY OF THIS BLOTTING PAPER, JUDY.

THE FLOWERS MUST BE AS FRESH AS POSSIBLE. SORT THEM INTO TWO GROUPS — THIN, DELICATE ONES AND THICK, JUICY ONES.

ARRANGE THE DELICATE ONES FIRST, JUDY. SEE THAT THE SPRAYS LOOK QUITE NATURAL.

BLOTTING PAPER

LEAVE ONE HALF OF THE BLOTTING PAPER FOR COVERING THE FLOWERS.

NOW FOR THE PRESSING.

PUT THE COVERED FLOWERS ON TO A SHELF OR TABLE WHERE THEY WON'T BE DISTURBED. COVER WITH A BOARD AND PILE SEVERAL HEAVY BOOKS ON TOP. DO THE SAME THING WITH THE SECOND GROUP AND LEAVE FOR 24 HOURS.

24 HOURS LATER...

TRANSFER THE FLOWERS CAREFULLY TO FRESH SHEET OF BLOTTING PAPER AND PRESS AGAIN. THE SECOND GROUP WILL NEED ONE MORE CHANGE OF BLOTTING PAPER AFTER THIS. LEAVE THEM ALONE FOR A WEEK THEN THE FLOWERS WILL BE DRY AND STIFF ENOUGH TO STICK INTO A BOOK.

I AM GOING TO MAKE THIS INTO A NATURE DIARY, MOTHER!

BUTTERCUP

GUM

MOTHER TELLS YOU HOW

To Decorate A Tray

MOTHER TELLS YOU HOW

TO MAKE A **GARDENING APRON**

MOTHER, WHAT CAN WE DO WITH THIS SACK?

WELL, YOU WANT A GARDENING APRON, JUDY, AND HERE'S YOUR CHANCE TO MAKE ONE.

WASH THE SACK WELL IN SOAPY WATER AND HANG IT UP TO DRY.

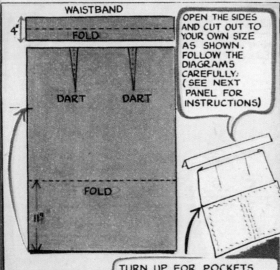

WAISTBAND

FOLD

4"

DART   DART

FOLD

11"

TURN UP FOR POCKETS

OPEN THE SIDES AND CUT OUT TO YOUR OWN SIZE AS SHOWN. FOLLOW THE DIAGRAMS CAREFULLY. (SEE NEXT PANEL FOR INSTRUCTIONS)

TIE END

1. HEM SIDES AND POCKET TOPS.
2. TRIM THE POCKETS WITH BRIGHT COLOURED RIC-RAC BRAID BEFORE MACHINING THEM TO THE APRON. SEW SOME MORE BRAID ON THE WAISTBAND.
3. MAKE DARTS TO FIT.
4. SEW ON WAISTBAND.
5. CUT STRIPS 2" WIDE AND 20" LONG FOR TIES AND SEW AT EACH END OF THE WAISTBAND.

OH, JUDY, YOU DO LOOK EFFICIENT. AND YOUR APRON'S SO SWEET, TOO!

MOTHER TELLS YOU HOW

TO GROW SWEET CORN

WE'LL PLANT OUR SWEET CORN TODAY, JUDY.

UNLESS YOU HAVE A GREENHOUSE OR FRAME IT IS BETTER NOT TO GROW CORN FROM SEED, BUT TO BUY PLANTS FROM A GOOD NURSERY.

THE HARDIEST KINDS TO GROW ARE "GOLDEN BANTAM" AND "JOHN INNES HYBRID". CHOOSE A SUNNY, SHELTERED POSITION FOR THE BED.

RAKE OVER THAT PLOT, JUDY, SO THAT THE SOIL IS QUITE FINE.

NOW WE'LL PLANT THE CORN A FOOT APART IN CIRCULAR GROUPS, NOT ROWS.

THIS IS VERY IMPORTANT AS SWEET CORN NEEDS AMPLE POLLINATION AND THE WIND HELPS TO DO THIS. KEEP THE SOIL WELL HOED ROUND THE PLANTS AND WATER AS NECESSARY.

HERE IS A FROST WARNING.

JUDY, RUN OUT AND PUT THE CLOCHES OVER THE SWEET CORN.

BE ON THE SAFE SIDE AND COVER THE PLANTS WITH CLOCHES OR GLASS JARS IF THERE IS FROST ABOUT.

THE COBS SHOULD BE READY BY AUGUST. CUT THEM WHEN THE GRAINS ARE STILL MILKY AND THE ENDS OF THE 'TASSELS' BEGIN TO TURN BROWN.

THE COB

STRIP AND COOK THE COBS IN FAST-BOILING, SALTED WATER UNTIL THE GRAINS ARE SOFT—TWENTY MINUTES USUALLY. SERVE WITH A DAB OF BUTTER ON EACH.

SWEET CORN IS BEST EATEN AS A FIRST COURSE AT LUNCH OR SUPPER.

MOTHER TELLS YOU HOW

To Make POT-POURRI

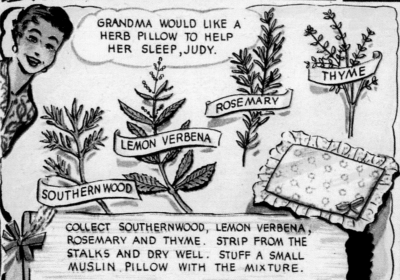

ADD A TEASPOONFUL OF ALLSPICE, ½ AN OUNCE OF CLOVES, A HANDFUL OF LAVENDER, 2 TABLESPOONSFUL OF POWDERED ORRIS ROOT AND A FEW BAY LEAVES. MIX WELL AND LEAVE IN A SHALLOW BOWL.

COLLECT SOUTHERNWOOD, LEMON VERBENA, ROSEMARY AND THYME. STRIP FROM THE STALKS AND DRY WELL. STUFF A SMALL MUSLIN PILLOW WITH THE MIXTURE.